ATTEMPTING
CHANGE

ATTEMPTING
CHANGE

ATTEMPTING
CHANGE

Teachers Moving
from
Writing Project
to
Classroom Practice

DAVID E. WILSON

Boynton/Cook Publishers
HEINEMANN
Portsmouth, NH

Boynton/Cook Publishers
A subsidiary of Reed Elsevier Inc.
361 Hanover Street
Portsmouth, NH   03801–3912

Offices and agents throughout the world

Library of Congress Cataloging-in-Publication Data
Wilson, David E., 1955–
    Attempting change : teachers moving from writing project to
classroom practice / David E. Wilson.
        p.   cm.
    Includes bibliographical references.
    ISBN 0-86709-340-4
    1. English language—Composition and exercises—Study and teaching (Secondary)—Iowa. I. Title.
LB1631.W49   1994
808'.042'0712—dc20   93–43848
                                                                          CIP

Editor: Peter R. Stillman
Production: Vicki Kasabian
Cover design: Mary Cronin
Printed in the United States of America on acid-free paper
98   97   96   95   94   CC   1   2   3   4   5

ATTEMPTING
CHANGE

Teachers Moving
from
Writing Project
to
Classroom Practice

DAVID E. WILSON

Boynton/Cook Publishers
HEINEMANN
Portsmouth, NH

Boynton/Cook Publishers
A subsidiary of Reed Elsevier Inc.
361 Hanover Street
Portsmouth, NH   03801-3912

Offices and agents throughout the world

We would like to thank the teachers who have given their permission to include material in this book. Every effort has been made to contact the copyright holders for permission to reprint borrowed material where necessary. We regret any oversights that may have occurred and would be happy to rectify them in future printings of this work.

Library of Congress Cataloging-in-Publication Data
Wilson, David E., 1955-
    Attempting change : teachers moving from writing project to
classroom practice / David E. Wilson.
        p.   cm.
    Includes bibliographical references.
    ISBN 0-86709-340-4
    1. English language—Composition and exercises—Study and teaching
(Secondary)—Iowa.   I. Title.
LB1631.W49   1994
808'.042'0712—dc20   93-43848
                                                                           CIP

Editor: Peter R. Stillman
Production: Vicki Kasabian
Cover design: Mary Cronin
Printed in the United States of America on acid-free paper
98   97   96   95   94   CC   1   2   3   4   5

in memory of
my grandmother
Helen Loretta Wilson
and my mother
Joyce Anne Wilson

Contents

Acknowledgments

I am indebted to Jerie Weasmer, my colleague and friend at Tipton High School. Jerie is passionate about learning and teaching; she insisted that I spend my summers at the Bread Loaf School of English or in the writing project; she—and students like Darren, Circe, and Jay—taught me how to be a teacher.

Attempting Change began as an undefined area of curiosity while I was in my final summer of study at Bread Loaf. A round of thanks, then, goes to Nancy Martin, who enthusiastically entertained my curiosity and helped me find definition. Equally important that summer was Shirley Brice Heath, who patiently helped me shape my questions then gave me a method for answering them.

The research for this book could not have been conducted without the cooperation of Jim Davis, director of the Iowa Writing Project, Cleo Martin, co-founder with Jim of the Project, and the teachers and students who generously agreed to answer my questions and allow me to peer over their shoulders. I was overwhelmed by their enthusiasm, support, and unselfish surrendering of their time. Robin, Wilma, Eileen, and Hal became my teachers; I continue to learn from them, and I continue to be grateful.

Gerald Hodges, John Conner, Jix Lloyd-Jones, and Jim Marshall provided support and assistance as I collected and reflected on my data, then drafted and redrafted my results for my dissertation at the University of Iowa.

Here in Nebraska I am indebted to colleagues and friends in the Center for Curriculum and Instruction and the Department of English who ply me with love, support, and guilt. In particular, Robert Brooke and Kate Ronald have spent long hours reading drafts, responding to them, and drinking coffee with me as I attempted to reenvision my work and better understand what I had seen. Joy Ritchie, too, has listened to endless tales of the Iowa Writing Project and has invited me inside the Nebraska Project.

From a distance Pat Scanlan, Marilyn Ohlhausen, Mary Beth Hines, and Bonnie Sunstein have offered their support and encouragement by way of e-mail, telephone, and the post. And Peter Stillman has provided generous extensions and helpful responses in his role as editor.

And throughout it all, David Smith has been ever-present, ever-patient as I worked to finish this project.

I thank you.

Preface

The writing project movement has proven to be very durable, but we have little research to suggest what specific changes these projects encourage in teachers' beliefs and practices. This book reports the results of surveys, interviews, case studies, and more than seventy hours of classroom observation with past participants in the Iowa Writing Project in order to describe the complex relationship between the teachers' practices and beliefs when they attempted to change their approach to the teaching of writing. (See the Appendix for more details on the research design.)

It tells stories, the stories of teachers like Robin, Wilma, Eileen, Hal, and the story of my own involvement with the writing project— first as a teacher/participant, later as a facilitator, and finally as a researcher.

Results of the study support the assertion that participation in the writing project had a strong influence on the beliefs and practices of the secondary English teachers of this study, but also indicate that the contexts of schooling served as an impediment to the implementation of their beliefs.

Project graduates believed that their teaching was greatly changed by their participation, and they valued the changes. Their articulated *beliefs* about writing and the teaching of writing were consonant with the general principles of the writing project movement. They especially seemed to believe in the importance of writing to learn, frequent student writing, and a positive environment for such writing.

These teachers' *practices* placed them in greatest consonance with the writing project principles in the frequency of student and teacher writing, the use of positive comments in response to student writing, and student ownership over topic choice. They claimed that such consonance is more likely in classes that are small, elective, upper level, or writing-centered.

Dissonance seemed to occur in the areas of grading, student ownership over due dates and revision, and the relative importance of "correctness." The teachers believed that such dissonance is caused by a variety of factors: too little time, too many students and class preparations, already-established curricula, students inexperienced in a process methodology, outsider expectations concerning writing instruction, and their own old habits and their mixed feelings about new ones.

In general, change seemed to be pushing these teachers in one direction while the contexts of schooling and old conceptions of teaching and writing pushed them in another.

Chapter One opens with the story of my involvement with the writing project then explores the history and design of the project in Iowa. It also introduces this study.

Chapters Two, Three, and Four explore much of what the writing project graduates said to me as they returned their questionnaires or sat with me on their front porches or in their kitchens or classrooms. Chapter Two addresses these teachers' reports of their beliefs and their change processes, Chapter Three explores their reports of their classroom practices, and Chapter Four steps back to make sense of the questionnaire and interview responses.

Chapters Five and Six move close to four teachers—Robin, Wilma, Eileen, and Hal—and into their classrooms. I spent a semester observing these four teach, interviewing them, reading their students' writing, and interviewing some of their students. Chapter Five introduces the teachers then explores their "successful" practices, that is, those that seemed to represent well their intentions. Chapter Six examines the points of dissonance and difficulty, the practices that did not seem to follow from their stated beliefs.

Robin, Wilma, Eileen, and Hal—the four case study teachers— authored Chapter Seven. Here they reconsider their professional lives before and after the writing project, think about what it meant to be a case study subject, and tell the stories of their classroom lives since then. Hal's story runs throughout and is punctuated by the voices of Robin, Eileen, and Wilma.

Chapter Eight steps back from the study, reviewing some of what was discovered and exploring how change was both promoted and impeded for these teachers.

All names of the study participants are pseudonyms, and many potentially identifying details of geography have been changed to protect their privacy.

Chapter One

Coming to Know the Writing Project

Beginnings

Writing. I suspected students hated it. And I knew that I, as an English teacher, certainly hated teaching it. I dodged it whenever possible. No time to have the students write. Too busy with literature, spelling, vocabulary, grammar, usage, and punctuation. How could I expect my kids to write if they didn't know the difference between a subject and a verb?

So, I busied myself and my students with wonderful lessons on the parts of speech (complete with appropriate worksheets) and sometimes we talked about topic sentences. But we never made it around to writing.

Then, one summer I moved from Pennsylvania to Iowa to take a new position at Tipton High School, and that August when the secretary handed me my class schedule, my heart skipped a beat: two sections of Composition I and another two of Advanced Comp? No escaping it now; I'd have to teach writing.

I frantically searched through the files I had inherited from my predecessor, hoping to find a course outline or curriculum guide. Nothing.

Text books. There has to be a classroom set of *Warriner's* around here, I thought. I dug through the cabinets in the English office. Again, nothing.

I was slumped in a chair, nursing a cup of cold coffee, when Jerie Weasmer, my new department chair, walked into the room. "Are you ready for them?" she asked.

"Not yet. It's those comp classes. I can't find the *Warriner's*."

"*Warriner's*?" she asked, eyebrows raised. "I threw those out last year."

"They were old?"

1

"No, just dangerous. What do you want with *Warriner's* in a writing class?"

And so we talked. I talked about units in punctuation, usage, and vocabulary; she talked about peer response, freewriting, and throwing out the texts. My panic intensified. What a liberal.

"But how can they write if they can't even punctuate correctly?"

"Trust them. Give them a chance. Besides, who says they can't write?"

Can't write? Why, everybody knows they can't write. Even *Newsweek* says they can't write. Trust them? Sure I'll trust them. I'll trust them to use up all the red ink this school has on hand.

But Jerie persisted. She talked about SIWP, the Southeast Iowa Writing Project, and how it had helped her to think in different terms about teaching writing. "You really ought to take the Project," she said. "I used to try the same things you're talking about, Dave, but it doesn't work. Tell me that all of your worksheets have made a better writer out of any of your students."

She had me there. We talked some more, I gave a little, and she sent me home with a copy of Ken Macrorie's *Uptaught.* Later that fall Jerie took me to a language arts conference in Des Moines to hear Macrorie speak; the next summer she provoked me to go to the Bread Loaf School of English at Middlebury College to study with him. And throughout it all she continued to talk about the Project, introducing me to other Eastern Iowa teachers who had participated in this inservice program.

Sandra Bolton taught down the road at Mt. Vernon. Lin Buswell was over at Iowa Valley. Tom Handlen taught in Davenport. They all shared an enthusiasm for this writing project that made me uncomfortable. Given my recent experience in an all-day staff development program entitled "Soil Conservation Across the Curriculum," I was particularly skeptical about staff development. No inservice program, in my experience, had ever been as valuable or as life-changing as this writing project was painted to be. And I didn't much trust that life-changing talk. These folks had a vocabulary—*process, ownership, draft*—and a set of rituals—peer response, green ink, journals—that seemed to identify them as an in-group and me as an outsider. Too much of the cult there for my tastes.

But they also shared an enthusiasm and an excitement for writing and teaching writing that intrigued me. When together, they'd swap success stories; they'd talk about how Amy or Tim or Louise had written a piece that had moved them and their students to tears or anger or joy. It was a kind of talk that I hadn't often heard in my tenure as a teacher, and from teaching next door to Jerie, I knew that it wasn't just talk. Her students—unlike mine—*were* excited about writing. They wrote, and they wrote well.

And so it was in the summer of 1982 that I found myself in the Southeast Iowa Writing Project seated around a circle of tables with twenty-five other teachers from various school districts in Eastern Iowa. Jim Davis and Cleo Martin, co-founders of the Project, were our facilitators. We met for three weeks in a large room in Iowa City that had been rented by the Grant Wood Area Education Agency, Jim Davis' employer.

On the first morning Jim worked at getting us acquainted with one another. I was a little annoyed when I learned that sixteen of my classmates were elementary teachers. What could we possibly have in common? They'll probably want to talk about bulletin boards, I mused. My doubts about this project returned.

We did some reading, I don't recall now just what, and we broke into small groups for discussion. Jim, slyly, was introducing us to a pattern that would become quite familiar over the next three weeks: some whole-group work, some small-group work, some individual work, then back to small groups, then a final return to the whole group before lunch. Each morning from 8:00 to 11:00, we'd read, write, and talk about writing and the teaching of writing. Jim presented each of us with two bibliographies: one listed in categories the books available in the room for our use; the other listed in the same categories the articles we'd be receiving throughout the three weeks. We'd be studying concepts of the writing process, generating student writing, responding to student writers, establishing sequences of writing experiences, assessing and the writing program, and writing across the curriculum.

After lunch Cleo worked at getting us more familiar with one another. Our afternoon sessions would run from noon to 3:00, she explained, and would be spent writing and sharing our writing. On Mondays, Wednesdays, and Fridays we'd meet to share our writing; on Tuesdays and Thursdays we were free to write wherever we desired. Our quiet, air-conditioned room would always be available for writing, and Cleo would be there if we needed assistance.

Then Cleo, too, made a sly move. She invited us to take a few minutes to informally write a response to "the plan" for these next three weeks. "The Plan is good," I announced in my opening sentence, "I like The Plan." After ten or fifteen minutes, Cleo invited us to share our thoughts. My new colleagues, secondary and elementary teachers alike, seemed, like me, to be drawn to the order and flexibility suggested in Jim and Cleo's descriptions of our time together. It looked as though there might be room for each of us in the plan.

As we spoke up, Cleo listened intently, nodded approvingly, and remained silent. Later she suggested that she'd like very much to read what we'd written, and we placed our papers in the collection box she'd introduced for that purpose. With little fear or fanfare, we had already written and shared our first papers. Again, we had slipped into what would become a comfortable pattern.

And so, after two years of hearing about the Project, I was quickly becoming an insider. I had assumed the first of three roles I would eventually assume in relationship to the writing project: student, teacher, and researcher.

The Writing Project

The founders of the Bay Area Writing Project, which was begun in 1973 in Berkeley, believed that teachers who were given the opportunity to write, to share their work with colleagues, to study recent composition theory and research, to reexamine their own classroom practice, and to develop their own plans for improved instruction would become more effective teachers.[1]

Since 1973, the Bay Area Writing Project has spawned the National Writing Project, with more than one hundred affiliated sites around the United States and abroad. In addition, other states, agencies, colleges and universities, and school districts have established their own independent writing projects. Most draw from the same research and theoretical base (Vygotsky 1962; Moffett 1968, 1981; Britton 1970; Macrorie 1970; Emig 1971; Elbow 1973; Britton et al. 1975; Graves 1983), a base that sees writing as a creative process of immense perceptual, linguistic, and cognitive complexity in which meanings are made through the active and continued involvement of the writer with the unfolding text. James Moffett (1981, 81) refers to this movement as "the most positive development in English education . . . during the whole period since World War II . . . ; [it has] accomplished far more good than all of the U.S. Office of Education Project English curriculum centers of the '60s put together."

Iowa's writing project was in its fifth year when I enrolled; it had begun in the summer of 1978 as the Southeast Iowa Writing Project (SIWP). Given both local funding and a local history of sponsoring similar institutes, Iowa's project founders elected to remain independent of the National Writing Project. The SIWP's sponsoring institution, the University of Iowa, had offered several National Defense Education Act English institutes in the 1960s and had developed special institutes for junior and senior high school teachers on the teaching of composition.

Since 1978 the SIWP has expanded beyond its original boundaries to become the Iowa Writing Project (IWP); in the years since its inception, more than six thousand teachers from all grade levels and content areas have studied in the Project's three-week summer institutes.

"The institute design," says Project founder and director James S. Davis, "is driven by notions of learning rather than teaching."[2] In the mornings, the participants read from the current research and theory on writing and writing instruction. Each site makes books from the Project library available to the participants; in addition, articles are photocopied. Especially popular in 1982 were Peter Elbow, Donald Graves, and Donald Murray. Currently, participants seem drawn to Nancie Atwell, Lucy Calkins, Linda Rief, and Tom Romano.

Davis sees this reading as "issue provocation. 'Do the ideas of this author make sense to you, given your reality of teaching?'"[3] Control and time are generally given to the workshop participants. They are free to direct their own reading so that it most clearly addresses their own particular contexts, and they are provided workshop time to do that reading, to make sense of it in writing, and to talk about it with their co-participants. The combination of the teachers' experiences and the reading provides the stimulus for dialogue.

In the afternoons the participants become writers. Working from a "personal narrative writing base,"[4] the teachers write, read, and respond to one another's writings and talk about their processes and products. This component of the Project design, believes Davis, ". . . may be more important than the morning. It grounds the morning."[5] Moffett (1981, 81) and the Bay Area Writing Project founders seem to agree. "'If teachers are ever going to teach writing more and teach it better, they will have to produce more writing themselves.' . . . Surely, a major reason that many teachers ignore, slight, or mangle the teaching of writing is that they lack direct experience with the learning issues entailed in writing."

The afternoon sessions, then, attempt to provide the participants with that direct experience and with a workshop model for writing instruction. The instructor provides time and encouragement for writing, responds orally and in writing to the participants' efforts, introduces them to a variety of forms of peer response, and periodically provokes some reflection on and discussion of what the participants are learning about themselves as writers. At the end of the project, a collection of the teachers' writings is published.

These three-week summer institutes are now referred to as Level I of the Iowa Writing Project. Since the development of these institutes, three nonsequential follow-up programs have been designed and implemented at teacher-participant request. Level II, the second to be developed but not necessarily the second program a teacher might take, is a two-week summer institute, similar in format to Level I, that allows Level I graduates to study further in an area of particular interest such as response, revision, or assessment. Level III, the third to be developed, is a year-long journal-keeping seminar. Here Level I graduates engage in focused observation and record keeping of one of their classes, meeting biweekly with other teachers to receive support and discuss what they are discovering. The fourth program to be developed, a two-week workshop on writing and literature, allows teachers to explore the connections between teaching and learning writing and teaching and learning literature.

Levels I and II are taught by two-person teams; generally a pair of K–12 teachers who have taken the Project and have been invited by Davis to become facilitators. Level III is facilitated by one person, generally someone with experience as a Level I instructor. The writing and literature workshop, to date, has been taught by Davis alone. Davis selects all of the writing project instructors, looking for teachers who "have demonstrated real intellectual, teaching, and leadership strengths since their involvement in Level I and Level II or III."[6] Many of these people have regularly submitted proposals to conduct sessions at professional conferences and have continued their professional development by enrolling in graduate programs.

There is another component to the Iowa Writing Project: the annual fall conference. New Level I participants are strongly encouraged to attend the two-day conference, talk about their own writing, talk about their efforts at teaching or using writing in their classrooms, and receive support from their workshop classmates and other teachers. A keynote speaker—generally someone whose work the particpants will know from their own reading—is invited to address the group. Past speakers include Nancie Atwell, Glenda Bissex, James Britton, Lucy Calkins, Donald Graves, Nancy Lester, John Mayher, Nancy Martin, Miles Meyers, James Moffett, and Donald Murray. In addition, writing project graduates conduct break-out sessions to share aspects of their own teaching, and time is allotted for small-group discussions and peer response to one another's writing.

Working from a document composed earlier by Cleo Martin (1985), Jim Davis, Dick Hanzelka, and Cleo Martin, the three original Iowa Writing Project Steering Committee members, attempted to define what it is that the project fosters. They and their cadre of project instructors agreed that the following seven ideas are "central in the Iowa Writing Project and in the teaching of writing":

1. Writing can enhance learning in all areas of the school curriculum, at all levels. Writing is a way of creating meaning and of discovering what one knows.

2. Students need to write regularly and in varied contexts in order to become better writers. Teachers who themselves write regularly are likely to be credible when they advise students about the writing process and about the values of writing.

3. Writers need to know and care about what they write. Writers need to have ownership of their own processes and products. The knowledge used for writing should at least in part be based on the students' own experiences. The topics students write about should be negotiable.

4. Some people can write with ease, regularity, and joy—just as some people can talk with ease, regularity, and joy. Confidence is essential if people are to do this. An increase in confidence often means an increase in competence.

5. Writers of all ages need readers to respond to their work at various stages. In schools, students and teachers can serve that function; audiences beyond the school can be easily accessed as well. When facilitating the sharing of student writing, it is important to remember that writers can benefit more from positive than from negative comments on their writing.

6. Writing is a complicated process. Classroom experience needs to include time for all components of the writing process— composing, drafting, revising, editing, publishing, and reflecting on the process itself. It is sometimes tempting to give disproportionate attention to editing. Some student writing needs to go through revision and editing—some doesn't.

7. Writing occurs in a wide variety of contexts in a wide variety of forms for a wide variety of purposes. There is no such thing as a formula for "good" writing that will operate in all contexts.

These seven ideas, then, make up the framework of principles for the Iowa Writing Project, a framework, though never spelled out so directly, that became quite familiar to me by the end of my third week in the Project. Similar ideas operate in other writing projects around the country.[7]

Do writing project participants adopt these principles? Do these ideas make a difference in their classroom practices? Moffett must think so. As mentioned earlier, he has written of all the "good" they have done. Daniels and Zemelman (1985, 4) claim that " . . . a gratifying percentage of our [Illinois Writing Project] teacher-participants have significantly improved their classroom teaching skills. . . ." Locally, too, there is a belief in the value of these projects. In case studies of Iowa Writing Project participants that were conducted in 1979–80, one participant-teacher stated, "The SIWP changed my attitudes. . ., [it] was valuable for me. . . ."[8] Her principal agreed: "I think she was a good teacher before, but she has been helped a lot by the Project . . ., and our kids have benefited from her being involved in the Project."[9] A case study of another teacher, Sandra Bolton, my friend from down the road, went even further: "Although, after ten years of teaching, she was at the same school, teaching the same courses, she was not the same teacher she had been before SIWP. . . ."[10] The Project was "a 'shot in the arm' for her, she maintained. It had come along after ten years of teaching and given her new perceptions into the writing process, and the methodology needed to translate her perceptions into classroom reality."[11] It seems that writing project graduates, their administrators, and outside observers are convinced—at least in some cases—of the value of participation in the writing project.

Indeed, my own experience in the writing project persuaded me of its value. By the last week I was even pleased that so many of my new colleagues were elementary teachers. It had been the first time I had ever been asked to work with teachers below grade seven, and I found them to be more interested in children than bulletin boards. In fact, their insistent focus on the child provided a necessary counterbalance to the secondary teachers' preoccupation with skills and standards.

The project also seemed to have persuaded my new colleagues of its value. During our last week together we selected pieces for our class publication, *Emergences*, got a final round of peer response to assist us in last-minute revisions, then received some help in editing. I chose "Damned Admirable," the story I'd written about my decision to join the Peace Corps. LuAnn selected a memorable piece about a thin, bony child she'd met at a check-out counter; Marty wrote an "Earth Poem"; Wilma selected her piece about her daughter and her grandmother. Robin submitted two pieces, the second entitled "Journal Reflections." It seemed to sum up the way many of us felt that last week.

> I feel as though I have so much to say—not right this minute exactly—but sometime. Stories of my life and family that I want to preserve on paper—like so many of the things I've already written have. I so hope that I'll continue writing after the course is finished—I think I will—I think I'll have to—I owe it to ME to keep writing—it's my lifeline, my sanctuary, my friend.
>
> I can't help but wonder what will become of us all. Oh, I know we'll supposedly meet in October for the conference or workshop or whatever—but what if someone can't come?
>
> These people have touched my life—I've shared things with them that I might not share with my closest of friends. Why? What is this mystical bond between us that allows us, prompts us to spill

our guts—to strip away the outer layers that protect our innermost thoughts? I trust them. I know them. They're like me in many ways—sensitive to others—the feelings—the emotions—whether we evoke laughter or tears—we reach one another.

We help one another grow. We motivate one another and thrive.

I'll miss them.

I'll miss their stories, their sharing of experiences, their smiles, their laughter, even their theoretical suggestions.

They've stretched my mind—they've helped me find ME.

How do you thank them and how do you thank Cleo and Jim for making it the kind of class that was truly an *EXPERIENCE*?

The writing comes easier now—more naturally than ever—good or bad—it's me and I write for *me* but *you* have helped me to do that.

If I can do that for my students—

help them to write for themselves and love it—feel at home in it—

that is my goal

that is my dream.

WRITING—what a beautiful word.

What a beautiful group of people to share it with.

Post-Project Experiences

I returned to school that fall newly excited about writing and teaching, and I attempted to refine the workshops I had instituted after my earlier summer at the Bread Loaf School of English. My students—like Jerie's—became more excited about writing. Liberated from a focus on spelling, punctuation, grammar, and form, they wrote and they wrote well. Darren did it when he wrote about his parents' divorce. Circe did it in her piece about visiting her grandmother in a nursing home. Jay did it in his story about a memorable KISS concert. And I did it, too, when I began to write and share my own writing with them and their classmates. The school's supply of red ink was no longer in danger.

I was fortunate. The environment for my attempts at change was fertile. I had spent that earlier summer at Bread Loaf with Ken Macrorie. And I had some collegial support; next door Jerie was attempting to build a similar classroom. Our doors, in fact, were side by side, making quick conferences easy. I also had administrative support; our principal had attended my writing project on visitor's day, and, as a result, volunteered to limit enrollments in composition courses to twenty. In addition, when one set of parents angrily questioned my methods, the principal announced to them that "Mr. Wilson has a great deal of research to support his approaches."

The home economics teacher, who had always made generous use of writing in her classes, welcomed our suggestions about substituting an I-search paper[12] for the formal research paper she generally assigned and about incorporating peer response. And one of the science teachers asked for and implemented our advice on using more informal writing in his classes.

It wasn't all easy, but it was more exciting than any teaching I had ever done before. The straight-A students seemed to have the most trouble adjusting to my attempts at liberating them, and they were often vocal in their displeasure. The basketball coach thought it sounded like all play and no work. Discouraging words from any of them often set me to doubting. Fortunately, Jerie provided ample support and encouragement, and my students—like Darren and Circe—provided evidence of success: more writing, better writing, and more varied writing than I had ever thought possible.

I also continued to receive support from my project classmates. Robin and I, both responsible for our schools' journalism programs, ran into one another at conferences for yearbook and newspaper students and advisors. In addition, we periodically exchanged phone calls in our attempts at sorting out how we might make our deadline-driven journalism classes more compatible with our now process-oriented composition classes. And most all of us from that summer project showed up for the writing project conference that fall. We embraced upon first spotting one another and quickly got word around to meet that evening in the room that Marty and I were sharing. There we swapped success stories, writing—our students' and our own—and encouragement. And we called Kelly and Bob, two of our missing compatriots, to persuade them to join us the next day. This reunion with writing project classmates, the presentations by other writing project graduates, and the words of wisdom from speakers Karen Pelz and Jim Davis provided a substantial dose of support and encouragement and propelled me back into my high school classroom. It was emboldening to learn that I was now a part of a professional community—a movement—much larger than the small district in which I taught. I was an insider.

Two New Roles

The value of the writing project was reconfirmed for me when, several years later, I was asked to teach in the project. I moved into a dormitory room in a small, private college in Clinton, Iowa, and joined Tom Handlen as a member of a two-person teaching team. Tom, with several years' experience as a writing project instructor, took responsibility for the afternoon workshops. By then my enthusiasm for writing and teaching writing had perversely taken me to graduate school where I was eagerly reading everything I could find on writing. Given my familiarity with the research and theory, I took responsibility for the morning sessions. It was my job to introduce our participants to research and theory on writing and writing instruction, to help them direct their reading so that it addressed their individual needs and contexts, and to provide them with time to do the reading, to make sense of it in writing, and to talk about it with their colleagues.

It was a strange and exciting new role for me. On that first Thursday, as the participants wrote, I mused in my journal:

> Do these folks see me as I saw Jim and Cleo? Strange to think so. My professional growth—which began at Bread Loaf and in the writing project—has changed me. A new role, but still a learner. Am enjoying listening to these teachers, spending time with them. All are "experts."

That June was my second Iowa Writing Project, and I marveled at how closely it paralleled my first experience. A diverse group of teachers from a variety of grade levels, subject areas, buildings, and communities came together and created a community of their own. Many people who had at first resisted Tom's efforts to refer to them as writers, came by that third week to see themselves as writers. And I began to see that their new enthusiasm and community came in large measure from their work in the afternoon sessions, not from the morning sessions. On the eve of our last session together, I wrote in my journal:

> I've enjoyed this. Watching this group gel. Watching them process and show off their insights. They are proud of what they know and eager to share it. When they talk now, they sound truly concerned about the students. I'm curious. I want to peer into their minds and classrooms. I want to know what they know—what they've learned—where it will take them.

On the last day I said goodbye to Mercia and Jeanne and Jim and the others, then jumped in my car for the long drive to Vermont, where I had been returning for several summers to work on a master's degree in English at Bread Loaf. My mind wandered from the interstate to the teachers I had just left to the classes I'd be taking at Bread Loaf to my doctoral program at the University of Iowa where I was about to finish my coursework. I was going to need a research project for my dissertation, and somewhere in Ohio I determined that it ought to have something to do with the Iowa Writing Project—perhaps its effects. As both a participant and an instructor, I had added my voice to those—like Moffett—who felt the project helped classroom teachers enjoy a kind of success that few other inservice programs inspired. But I was curious. In what ways did the writing project influence its participants? I *did* want to peer into the minds and classrooms of those participants. What would I find if I asked teachers about the writing project, about their beliefs and practices in writing and the teaching of writing? What would I find if I followed Mercia, Jeanne, and Jim back into their classrooms? Would their post-project experiences be like mine? I was aware of the vague claims and informal reports about the value of writing projects in influencing teachers' beliefs and classroom practices, but I wanted to paint a clearer picture. I decided to add one more task to my list of things to accomplish at Bread Loaf: map out a dissertation research study. Given the presence of teachers and scholars like Nancy Martin, Dixie Goswami, Courtney Cazden, and Shirley Brice Heath, I couldn't imagine more fertile ground for the germination of such a project.

Designing a Study

I met first with Nancy Martin and expressed my desire to follow the Iowa Writing Project graduates back into their schools and classrooms in order "to construct a picture of English teaching and learning in a sample of writing project classrooms in secondary schools." Given advice and encouragement from her, I met with Goswami and Cazden, drew up a rough outline of a study, and then asked Shirley Heath to read and discuss it with me. By the time I had graduated and left Bread Loaf that summer, I had a proposal and a plan that pleased both me and my Bread Loaf mentors. Back at Iowa I met with Jim Davis to receive his blessing, then I polished my proposal with help from my committee.

My curiosity and experience, then, led me to ask the question: In what ways has participation in the Iowa Writing Project had a continuing influence on secondary English teachers who have studied in the Iowa Writing Project? Four specific questions would guide the research:

1. As determined from questionnaires distributed to all 1982 and 1985 Iowa Writing Project participants who teach secondary English, what is their assessment of the influence which participation in the IWP has had on their teaching?

2. As determined from interviews with twenty questionnaire respondents, why have these teachers responded as they have concerning the influence which the IWP has had on their teaching?

3. What evidence will the case studies (of four teachers selected from the larger sample) reveal of the continuing influence of the IWP?

4. What relationships can be found between the four case study teachers and the larger sample regarding the influence that participation in the IWP had on their teaching?

My questions, then, reflected a three-part methodology: questionnaires, interviews, and case studies. (See the Appendix for a more detailed explanation of this methodology.) Each step in the methodology moved closer to the experiences—the lived lives—of individuals in an attempt to paint greater detail into my portrait of post-project teachers. The questionnaires, I hoped, would give me some broad sense of writing project graduates, their beliefs, their practices, their change processes. The interviews would place me face-to-face with twenty of those teachers, and would allow me to get to know them better and to ask the kinds of questions that might be raised by their questionnaire responses. And the case studies would take me into the classrooms of four of those interviewees and would help me understand their practices and the contexts for those practices.

In order to better understand the beliefs and assumptions on which the Iowa Writing Project was based, I met with Jim Davis, Dick Hanzelka, and Cleo Martin, the three original Iowa Writing Project Steering Committee members. We sat at a large booth in an Interstate 80 truckstop, drank coffee, and attempted to define what it is that the writing project fosters. The seven principles presented earlier were the result of our two-hour session. Later I took these principles to a meeting of project instructors for their input and approval. My intention was to use these principles as a kind of template for what I'd be hearing and seeing.

Wanting to conduct my case studies in the fall, I elected to send out my questionnaires in late spring and hoped to gain a return in time to conduct the interviews over the summer and early fall. In moving from a skeptical outsider to a curious insider, I had assumed my third role with the writing project; I was becoming a researcher.

Notes

1. H. Daniels and S. Zemelman, *A Writing Project: Training Teachers of Composition from Kindergarten to College.* (Portsmouth, NH: Heinemann, 1985) 3.

2. J. S. Davis, Personal communication with author, 17 February 1987.

3. Ibid.

4. Ibid.

5. Ibid.

6. Ibid., 13 December 1990.

7. H. Daniels and S. Zemelman, 13.

8. D. Bunch, *A Case Study: Kay Van Mantgen* (Unpublished manuscript, 1980b) 8.

9. Ibid., 4.

10. D. Bunch, *A Case Study: Sandra Bolton* (Unpublished manuscript, 1980a) 2.

11. Ibid., 7.

12. K. Macrorie, *Searching Writing* (Rochelle Park, NJ: Hayden, 1980).

Chapter Two

Teachers Talk About Their Teaching: Changes in Beliefs

As the questionnaires came back, I eagerly read them, took notes, and began to identify the twenty teachers for my interviews. To my surprise, only one teacher turned down my request for an interview. She wrote:

> I am sorry, but I will not be able to meet with you. I cannot afford to give up my forty-five-minute prep period during the day, and after 4:00 P.M. is a bad time for me. I have a thirty-minute drive one way to school, and my husband and I have two thousand acres to farm (including livestock). Good luck, and I hope you find more cooperation from others.

Indeed, despite these teachers' busy lives and multiple commitments, I did find remarkable cooperation—both with the questionnaires and the interviews. They returned the questionnaires promptly, often with lengthy responses to my open-ended questions. And although I had never previously met most of them, they invited me into their homes and classrooms for interviews, surrendering precious summer days and planning periods.

The interview with Laura, though perhaps dramatic, was representative of the reception I received. I found her in the school auditorium during the last period of the day. She was overseeing the final dressing of the stage for that evening's opening of the school play, which she was directing. She showed no dismay at my arrival and quickly ushered me up to her classroom where we talked for almost three hours in spite of my protestations that I didn't want to steal too much of her time. "I'm so glad you're here," Laura insisted, "because I haven't talked to anybody about what I'm doing in a long time." She answered my questions, asked many of her own, and pulled out student folders to illustrate the kind of writing she was getting. When I left, Laura had just enough time to race home, prepare a quick supper for her family, and return for the school play. I felt guilty for having stolen so much of her time, but the following week she wrote me a letter thanking me for *my* time, offering further assistance, and wishing me luck in my research.

I felt quite honored and overwhelmed by the responses of these teachers. Their eagerness to talk about their teaching was, for me, strong evidence of their commitment and their isolation.

Chapters Two, Three, and Four explore much of what these teachers said to me as I read their written responses or sat with them in their homes or classrooms, searching for the ways in which their involvement in the writing project may have influenced them. As I reviewed their questionnaires and the transcripts of our interviews, I found that their talk fell into three general categories: their beliefs about writing and the teaching of writing, their change processes, and their classroom practices. This chapter will address these teachers' reported beliefs and change processes; the following chapter will explore their reported practices; and Chapter Four will step back and make sense of the questionnaires and interviews.

Teacher Beliefs

As teachers reported their beliefs about writing and the teaching of writing, those beliefs were, for the most part, consonant with those that are central to the writing project. Questionnaire respondents were asked to articulate what they "believe about writing and the teaching of writing." Some of their responses to this question were brief, as was Kay's, who wrote, "Writing helps students to think and to learn." Other teachers, like Owen, wrote extended credo statements:

> I believe that writing is a cumulative process. I think that it is important to teach writing in connection with literature and speaking because the three elements combine to form the communication process. . . . It is too easy to isolate one aspect and thus lose perspective.
>
> I also do believe that writing is an ongoing process. Through continued writing, one grows as a writer. Through limited writing, one is held back. I like to focus in on individual viewpoints and experiences. I think it is only through this type of writing that *honest* communication takes place. I like to let my students think that a part of what writing is about is discovering their own ideas, thoughts, and emotions on paper. The written word is not only

communication with others, but it is also a visible communication with the self.

I have grown to believe there is no right way of writing. We, as teachers, have an obligation to show and expose individuals to different styles, techniques, and even tricks. But in the end, it is the student—the individual—who must decide what works best for him or her in the expression of his or her ideas. Although the writer grows through audience feedback, writing remains an individualized process adapted by and for the individual.

Most of the responses were in similar harmony with the writing project principles. Indeed, each of the seven statements was mentioned several times in the responses to this item in the questionnaire.

A variation on the second principle was the belief most frequently mentioned by the respondents. "The more practice there is, the better the writing will be," Marty wrote. Joan agreed: "Writing improves as one writes." And a third teacher elaborated: "If you want to learn to write, you must write. If you want to improve your writing, you must write and write and write some more." One-third of the respondents said that they believed that students need to write often, but few mentioned one of the other components of that second principle: Teachers, too, need to write regularly.

Almost an equal number of respondents wrote of writing as learning and discovery, a belief that put them in harmony with the first project principle. Writing "both *shapes* thinking skills and *is shaped by* our thinking processes," explained Sue. Nicholas believed that "writing is thinking and thinking is learning, clarifying, and expanding your personal world." They wrote of writing as "physical evidence of thinking," "a process of developing and discovering thought," and "one of the few ways to involve students in what they are learning."

Almost as popular was the belief that positive response to student writing and a positive environment are necessary for the student's development as a writer. "Their writing should be shared with people outside of the classroom—and outside of the school—as much as possible," stated Cindy. Teachers must "use a *positive* approach in order to build the confidence of the writer" and develop "a feeling of freedom and acceptance." "Response to student writing should always be positive." These teachers' belief in the need for positive response is clearly consonant with the fifth writing project principle.

Another area of agreement among respondents concerned the role of the teacher in the teaching of writing. Some believed that "writing probably cannot be taught." Others wrote of the teacher as "guide," "coach," or "contributor, not just a grader." Matt suggested that:

> The teaching of writing may be the most rewarding of all teaching
> assignments despite its demands on the teacher's time. Its greatest
> reward is in freeing the teacher to create a learning environment
> rather than obligating the teacher to present a prescribed set of
> skills to be mastered. The role of the facilitator is the vehicle for
> freeing the teacher to allow students to teach themselves. . . . There-
> fore, the more I can remove myself from the learning process, the
> better a teacher of writing I become.

Of course, not all teachers agreed with Matt, nor were all of their
beliefs in complete consonance with the seven writing project principles. The biggest area of dissent came in the importance of "correctness" in student writing. While some teachers wrote of "teaching
the correctness of writing through students' writing" and claimed
that "grammar study is accomplished very well through the editing
process," others were not so sure. "I believe that being positive works
BUT mistakes must be pointed out and corrections learned," said
Mary Lou. Marian, a ninth-grade teacher, believed that "more
emphasis has to be placed on the 'correctness' (spelling, grammar,
usage)." Patricia announced that she was "from the 'old school' to
the extent that spelling, usage, and sentence structure do make a difference. It's difficult to teach writing to someone who can't write a
complete sentence."

For the most part, then, these teachers' stated beliefs were in
consonance with all seven writing project principles. The teachers
especially seemed to believe in writing as learning and discovery and
in the importance of frequent student writing and of creating a positive environment for such writing. As a part of such an environment, they believed in the use of positive response to affirm their
students' writing. The area where we see the most dissonance
between some of the respondents' beliefs and the seven principles is,
again, in that area of "correctness" and its relative importance.

Several of the teachers spoke of beliefs and practices almost as
though they were one, as though they could not separate them. Joan
even said so: "You can't separate my philosophy from the way I
teach . . .; they're synonymous with one another." Many of the teachers, as they spoke of their beliefs about writing and the teaching of
writing, began to suggest the practices that they believed were
implied by these beliefs. Hal is one example:

> I believe the student learns to write by writing. And that you have
> to back off and let the student write. Create the atmosphere to make
> the student want to write. . . . I think for me it's response. It's the
> response that I give to their initial papers . . . . And so I assign so
> many writings in a quarter that kids have to do, but that's where it
> ends. I don't assign any topics or length or anything like that. And

they write at first because they've got to get the grade. And then once I start responding to them, then most of them—not all of them—will open up and will start to write things. That's when things start to happen. And that's hard to explain to people who haven't been through the course. That they learn to write by writing. You don't have to structure the whole lot for them. . . . I believe you don't have to mark all the grammatical mistakes and all that type of stuff. I still have lessons that we go through and we do grammar and that type of thing—mechanics. But I do that more to satisfy administration and parents, because I think you have to satisfy that facet too. And I don't do any of that with their writing. I don't mark any corrections at all. And it just amazes me—you have people who haven't been to the project who don't believe me—don't understand when I say that as the year goes on I get fewer and fewer grammatical mistakes. They clean themselves up. They just do. And especially when you get to publication time. Kids'll clean that stuff up. I just don't have to deal with that much anymore. It's an amazing phenomenon the way it works.

Hal and others expressed a strong belief in the importance of positive response for the development of their students as writers. In addition, Hal suggested a sequence of practice for his classes that is set in motion by the deliberate use of positive response to initially assigned student writing. Hal also claimed that such a sequence eliminated the need for direct instruction in "grammar and that type of thing," yet he still taught them to "satisfy" others. It would seem that occasionally Hal was engaging in practices in which he didn't believe, that it was not only his beliefs and allegiance to writing project principles that were informing and directing his practice.

Teacher Change

The Impetus for Change

All twenty teachers I interviewed, except for Lisa who was sent by her superintendent, participated in the writing project of their own volition. Their reasons for doing so were fairly uniform. Matt explained his:

First, it was four graduate credit hours that my school district was willing to pay for, and secondly, . . . the teacher next door to me at the high school had taken it . . . and made so many changes right away the next year, and she shared those changes with me and we talked off and on during the year about them. She's close enough to retirement age that I felt that if this has had this much impact on her, then it's something maybe I should look into. And I was getting kind of bored with the things I was doing. I think I was probably looking for a change about that time anyway. I didn't go into the writing project with that idea that . . . I'm going to have this big monumental change, but I was kind of restless.

Matt gave three reasons for participating in the writing project that resonated with those given by others: His district paid for the course; he had heard good things about the course; he was tired and ready for some change. In addition, other teachers spoke of having a need and hoped that the writing project could meet that need. Susan said:

I wanted to teach writing better and I didn't know how. I really did not have a way to teach writing effectively. I saw kids making a lot of mistakes grammatically. I saw kids who hated to write. And I didn't know how to change that.

Many of the teachers referred to what they perceived as poor preparation to teach writing. Betty explained:

I was an undergraduate in 1964 and back then no one taught you how to write. I had a course in expository writing and that was the sum total of my writing experience in college, and these people [who had taken the writing project] seemed to be having lots better results with what they were doing than . . . [I was].

The Process of Change

Across the board all of the teachers I interviewed reported changes in their beliefs about writing and the teaching of writing. It was a change process that generally began during the three-week workshop. Marilee, a woman who had taught in rural Iowa for twenty years, described it:

Maybe the first week you're just trying to climb over the wall that's in your head. We've been trained one way. We've had such a tremendous amount of experience in one way of teaching composition, and when suddenly somebody says, "Take a look at that wall that you've been using in defense of your writing strategies up until now," we don't want to bring that wall down. You don't want to say "I haven't been doing it the way I should have been doing it." So the first week you're just trying to get over the wall. By the second week you're in a deep ocean, and my God there are so many wonderful things out there in the ocean, and you can't catch the fish. . . . You truly search your entire professional training, your experience. You're going home and you can't rest with it. You are wondering, and you keep reading, and the more you read the more you realize you've got to shake loose from your past. I think it's a very difficult transition. Now by the third week of the project, it seems like that conversion has happened. Where all at once you begin to see a new shape, a new vision. You begin to get more concrete ideas of how you could do it. But that uncertainty continues . . . for . . . at least one year and . . . for some people three or four years.

Marilee identified resistance, conversion, and continued uncertainty as important steps in her change process, steps that resonated with those mentioned by other project graduates. Many of these teachers, in fact, used the metaphor of religious conversion. Betty claimed that "After going to the workshop, I was a completely different person." Matt spoke of being "changed, transformed." Rob left with "a different sense of myself, an ethical sense of myself." Such feelings of "new birth" were often accompanied by "a sense of euphoria" that left these participants "singing the praises of the project" and wanting to be "crusaders." Hal said that he and his fellow participants left feeling like "saviors." Marilee explained why she thought these religious metaphors were appropriate:

> [W]hen we came out of that writing project, it was like a whole new religion, a new philosophy, a new belief system, a new way of relating to one another. We became a community, just like a religious group becomes a community. We're working together for the same common destiny or fate—hoping for the same salvation, that we could survive as teachers. And, just like a religion gives you a whole different philosophy or attitude, I think the writing project gave you a vision that we didn't have until then, and turned, what had too often been drudgery, into almost a joy, at least a joyful way of looking at it.

As with some religious conversion, this change process was often perceived by the teachers as being dramatic—and even traumatic. One teacher talked about her "total turnaround." Others, as noted, cited a feeling of "new birth." Lisa spoke of going home each day of the workshop and crying, because, she said, "I had to reevaluate what I had done and make that comparison." Making that comparison—thinking about old practices—often involved some remorse. "Oh my god. It was just so shameful," Marilee claimed. Several spoke of wanting to apologize to former students. Rob, who taught at an urban school, said, "I cringe when I think back on some of the things I used to do."

Those "shameful" past practices usually sprang from a belief or assumption that writing was a product to be evaluated; that it arose from a conscious linear process, was a silent and solitary activity, was given to definite forms, and was best taught in steps: words, sentences, paragraphs, extended discourse. Correctness was paramount. For Rob this meant ". . . picking out all the spelling errors, mechanical things, taking papers apart." In Kate's junior high school classroom it meant "drill and skill—worksheet kinds of things." Only her "upper level" students were ever asked to write. Hal said:

> I'd always give assignments, and I'd always give the length of the paper, and I'd always check to make sure we had a topic sentence and supporting details. And I was always making sure all the punctuation was right and all the *t*'s were crossed and the *i*'s were dotted, and you know, the mechanical kind of stuff. And the papers were boring, and sad to admit, a lot of papers got lost because I didn't have time to read them or I didn't feel like reading them and it was easy to shove them off into the waste basket and say "Whoops." . . . And topics—I chose the topics.

Such assumptions placed these teachers within a more traditional paradigm of writing and writing instruction. For most teachers, the change process that brought them away from these kinds of assumptions continued after the project. Lisa identified four stages in her own change process—turmoil, exploration, excitement, and joy:

> While I was in the project and for the remainder of the summer after the project, . . . I went home and started looking at everything I was doing in all my courses and figuring how I was going to make that change for my classes, so it was still an upsetting process. Then the exploration was the first year. "By golly this does work. Now I wonder if this would work." Becoming sort of a learner along—checking against what I had learned in workshop, applying it to the students I had, [seeing] what I could handle, making judgments, giving up some things, changing others. I was really playing with what I knew and what I wanted to find out yet. The second year that excitement is "Oh, hey, I know now this is where I want to be. I'm getting good things out of it. How can I make it better? How can I evaluate what they're doing better?" Those types of things. Just making what I knew worked even more workable. . . . And that last one—this joy—is I know it even more. It does work. And it's also been a lot of giving up for me this year. . . . Where I really felt I could give up my agenda. I had, to some extent, before, but it was that last letting go I think because I had been in the classroom sixteen years before I had the first writing project. And I think just making that transition—I couldn't do it all at once and I gave it up in little pieces.

Lisa mentioned several points that were similar to those cited by other teachers. She spoke of the "upsetting process" of replanning practices, a sense of "playing with what I knew and what I wanted to find out yet," and the joyful realization that "it does work," that their students—like mine earlier—were writing with greater fluency, variety, and enthusiasm. In addition, Lisa and others made the point that it was difficult to make "that transition . . . all at once." Like Lisa, many of the teachers surrendered old expectations and shifted into new approaches "in pieces."

The Role of the Project in the Process of Change

When these teachers spoke of the writing project as a facilitator of their change, they seldom mentioned the research they had read. Rather, they spoke of "friendship," "camaraderie," "caring," and "closeness." Sheila explained that the project

> was a very emotional, very draining experience. . . . I think we just got so emotionally involved with each other, and we began to write about the things that really matter. You do a lot of crying as well as laughing.

Joan believes that the writing project was

> one of the closest environments that I've ever experienced in any educational process. And believe me, if every college professor taught their classes that way, I would not have failed statistics. And I wouldn't have, to this day, dreaded it. That's the way classrooms should be taught, and that's the premise I teach under. . . . That's what it transferred to me. It didn't even transfer the writing; it transferred a feeling. . . . That I counted. The feeling that they cared what I said and the feeling that I made a difference in their life and they made a difference in mine. Like a friendship or a relationship.

Hal claimed that the writing project works because it puts participants "through the process. . . . People don't sit there and say, 'This is the way it is,' or 'That's the way it works.' Believe me, they put you through it." Being "put through it" prompted Laura to rethink her practice: "I realized that what I wanted to write was what I wanted to write, not what somebody else wanted me to write about. And I figured, well, if that's how I felt about it, that's how the kids would feel about it." Wilma, too, referred to the afternoon sessions as being important in her change:

> I felt I improved but with very little dictatorial type teaching. It was almost like a gentle persuading or a tiny little suggestion that helped my work grow. Just by writing a piece and having someone respond to it, it moved me to revise it. The thing that just blows me away is how I improved by someone in a nurturing aspect as opposed to a gatekeeper. . . . It's almost like a mothering type thing. You feel very soothed. I send Cleo [the afternoon instructor] a card every Thanksgiving because she really showed me what true education is.

This process of change, then, struck most of these teachers as being most akin to religious conversion. It's no wonder that they framed it this way, given that they perceived this change as a surrendering of an old life, a shaking loose from the past, and an acquisition of "a new shape, a new vision," and a new "community." Innovations are acts of faith, and it would seem that these teachers could more easily hold such faith because they came to the Project of their own volition and with a perceived need, and because of the community, catharsis, and success they felt as students in the writing project, particularly in the afternoon workshops. As Rob said:

> When you go through the project you get this sense of community and you see this growth in your peers and it's not hard to imagine what the growth would be like in kids. And that's going to help you go back to the classroom more confidently and interject some of those same approaches.

The workshops, then, seem to have given the teachers a "sense of community," "friendship," "camaraderie," and "closeness." They also claimed that they left with "new belief system[s]" and new "approaches." Chapter Three, then, will address these teachers' approaches—their reported practices in the teaching of writing.

Chapter Three

Teachers Talk About Their Teaching: Changes in Practices

As these teachers wrote and spoke of their move from writing project to classroom practice, they mentioned their initial efforts at implementation, the role that support from others played in those efforts, the obstacles they encountered, their present practices, and their assessment of their post-project efforts at teaching writing.

Initial Efforts at Implementation

Not all of the teachers left the writing project with a clearly articulated belief system that they needed only to translate into practice. Rob explained:

> I don't think I had a philosophy after . . . [the writing project]. I had an approach . . ., a different approach to the teaching of writing. I only had a week by the time the project ended and school started. I think if I had had three or four weeks I might have reflected a little bit more and developed more of a philosophical basis for what I was going to do. As it was, I simply had an approach. It really didn't go any further than the kids should write what they want and that writing should be accepted and respected for what it is. . . . [Form and mechanics] should be left until the end. I just had those basics. It didn't allow me to reflect on what I was doing. It didn't give me anything to measure what I was doing against an ideal. . . . I couldn't stop and say, "Gee, I'm meeting my philosophical objectives here." I was sort of floating out there, and when that ran its

course, I didn't know where to go. I didn't have a basis to build on. I had an approach, and when that approach had run its course, I was done.

It wasn't until two years later that Rob began to solve his problem:

[Now] I don't try to recreate the project experience in my classroom like I did initially. I try to make it a more subtle part of my overall approach to teaching.... I've learned to use it a little bit better, instead of just doing it.

Many of the teachers began their post-writing project practice by "doing" the writing project in their classrooms—attempting to recreate the experience. Rob said that while that was "successful in many ways," it was also "frustrating" and "very tiring." "Maybe I was a little bit too idealistic," he admitted. His move from merely "adopting" the model to "adapting" it—integrating it into his classroom— allowed him to rest more comfortably. The passage of time seems to have allowed him to develop his new approach into a philosophy, an important step because such a philosophy provides a standard for decision making and self-assessment.

The mechanics of implementation—teachers' efforts at playing out their new beliefs—often caused concern for the teachers even before they moved back into their classrooms. Lisa spoke of being worried about "the very practicalities of it, ... the managerial aspects of running a writing workshop." Louise wanted "somebody to sit down and say, 'OK, day one you need to do this.'" Eventually "day one" arrived and "reality" came into play, said these teachers. LuAnn explained:

So you leave the project highly idealized. You've had this marvelous experience. Then fall comes and you're faced with reality.... It's so easy to lose the enthusiasm, because you get back into the classroom and you have the same things, you know. I mean a school day doesn't change because you've been in the project. You still have your seven- or eight-period day. You still have your grades.... You have to get out all those reports to parents. None of that changes.... So many of these things rub up against the concept of the project—of the spontaneity, the enthusiasm you're trying to generate. So when you get back in your classroom and the daily tasks, it's easy, at least it was for me, to lose the necessary strength and enthusiasm to carry out the concepts. It's easier to say, "All right, today we've read this story, now answer the ten questions at the end." That takes a lot less effort.

These teachers, then, left the writing project excited about an approach and were immediately confronted with the initial struggle of translating such an approach from one context to another. As Karla said, the writing project is not the "magic fix" to teachers' problems. They moved back into classrooms where the school day had not changed. Their problem, then, was not only one of translation—making sense of new concepts in old contexts, but also one of maintaining—as LuAnn said—the "necessary strength and enthusiasm to carry out the [new] concepts."

For some teachers it was not only school days that had not changed, but also colleagues. Robin found herself compromising as she attempted to implement her new beliefs into practice:

> After I took Level I, I started to let go, but I still had above me an English teacher who had been there for twenty years who taught the sophomores. Because I was teaching the freshmen, I knew I had to prepare them somewhat for his class, and he's a real grammarian. He concentrates on grammar and all of those things. His philosophy of course was different than mine was, but I still felt this need to prepare my kids somewhat for his classroom. So I still pulled out the *Warriner's* and we went through at least the parts of speech . . . [and] some basics of grammar. It was an isolated experience for the kids. It didn't seem to have connection to their writing. I felt a lot of struggle during that time. I was doing this and being sinful in doing it. I shouldn't be doing it. I felt like if the folks in Level I knew, they'd be throwing rotten tomatoes at me.

Robin was very aware of how her new beliefs differed from those held by colleagues. Although she no longer believed in the value of textbook instruction in grammar, she engaged in such practices because she knew that the sophomore English teacher would expect her freshmen to have studied grammar in that fashion, and she did not wish to penalize them. Such a practice felt "sinful" to Robin, recalling the language of religious conversion discussed earlier and suggesting that she felt she had violated an ideal or law. Her final sentence also suggests the perception of a writing project community, a community whose members hold certain beliefs and engage in certain practices, a community whose ideal Robin had transgressed. Eventually, with the support of colleagues in her Level III seminar, Robin "evolved to the point" where she exiled the grammar textbook to her shelf "as only a reference." Although she still occasionally worried that she wasn't adequately preparing her students for their sophomore English teacher, she believed her later practices more accurately reflected her beliefs. Robin's struggles to arrive at that point were aided by the support network she eventually found in her Level III seminar.

Obstacles to Implementation

Questionnaire respondents were nearly unanimous in identifying the major difficulty they had in "implementing the teaching of writing as fostered by the Iowa Writing Project" in all of their classes. As one teacher put it: "The biggest problem is the lack of time."

Teachers often noted the time it took to respond to student papers. "Time is my greatest enemy," Matt wrote. "By the end of a two-week cycle of folder assessment or reading journal response, I find myself cross and irritable and not the least interested in reading another word. If I weren't so convinced of the writing project model as a success, I would abandon it in a moment to ease the stress."

Sheer numbers of students and their papers also confounded teachers. Many of them felt compelled to read and respond to all that their students were writing. "Paper load is the single biggest headache," Judy stated. "When teaching in a small school, it's not uncommon to have five or six different preps with 100–150 students. Commenting on that much every night is mind-boggling and brain-draining." Susan was attempting to solve the problem by not asking "for as many papers as I want to because of lack of time. It's frustrating." Especially in courses with a broader language arts focus than just writing, teachers were having problems "finding the time to incorporate it into an already jam-packed curriculum." I "must allow time for grammar, literature, the research paper, the career unit . . .," explained Verla.

The length of a course and frequency with which it meets are also time factors. Some teachers complained that they only had their students for one semester, others that they only met with them every other day. The length of the class period, too, was seen by some teachers as an impediment. "I wish my classes were fifteen minutes longer to provide more time to write and share," wrote Eileen. This problem is only compounded by the number of students that might be taking a class. "Because of the size of my classes and the fact that I only see them for fifty minutes daily," explained Cindy, "I have difficulty finding time to conference with individuals as much as I would like to."

Students were another reported factor that often impeded their efforts at implementing a new approach within classrooms. Responses here fell in three areas: prior experience, expectations, and peer response.

Students "bring a ton of negative baggage about writing to class," Marilee stated. "It takes so long to move them into process writing. Implementing writing project concepts would be so much easier if all teachers preschool to secondary had a common expertise or at least a common understanding of how kids learn to write and how to help kids develop their writing." Instead, many of these teachers said that their students came up from lower grade levels where traditional school grammar was emphasized and classes were "so 'structured' that students had problems adjusting to a workshop atmosphere *and* thinking for themselves."

Given these backgrounds, students develop expectations about what should happen in an English class. Larry wrote of trying to de-emphasize "correct grammatical and punctuation errors in evaluating," but, he said, "I haven't actually followed through on this practice—at student request." "My students expect me to read, react to, and grade all their work," Rose explained.

Such backgrounds also cause problems for teachers who hope to implement peer response. Jake explained:

> Another problem I have . . . resides in the quality of student response to writing. Far too often I find students praising empty cli-chés, poorly wrought figures of speech, stereotyped character development, or absurd generalizations of their fellow students. I shouldn't be surprised because at times I found the same to be true among the adults in the writers' project itself. Perhaps even more disconcerting is the inability of students to recognize the more sophisticated and literary aspects of their peer's writing. I've been accused of snobbery on this account, but if the mediocre is praised and the excellent is ignored, what are we teaching? It seems to me that the teacher who relies on the use of student response must bear the responsibility to instruct his or her students to respond on a meaningful level. To be fair, in the past two years, I have noticed a significant improvement in student response to writing, probably because more teachers are incorporating student response in their teaching methods. Even so, teachers who give over to students the responsibility to respond to other students' writing are opening themselves up to the possibility that counterproductive commentary will be the result. Although I use peer response often and have seen many cases of its positive effects, I am uncomfortable with the knowledge that damaging peer response cannot be adequately controlled and is bound to occur.

Many others echoed Jake's concerns. They worry that students respond with a general "nice job" or simply echo the responses of others. And "when that happens I always feel like I need to respond too," Sally complained. They also complained of the "time needed to teach students to be effective responders for each other," and some mentioned that their students are reluctant to share their writing or to respond to others' writings orally.

Many of these teachers felt that outsider expectations were also impeding their efforts at implementation. They wrote of parents who were concerned about mechanics and principals who "require that most of our teaching time be devoted to grammar lessons from the text." Complained Sandy, "Parents and administration seem to feel that grammar is of utmost importance, and that all writing must be graded. More emphasis is placed on *how* something is expressed rather than *that* something is expressed." Sally found this particularly "disheartening" since her own district had "spearheaded an effort for the writing project." She added, "This difference in philosophy has led me to resign my position."

Jake believed that, "In this age of outcomes-based education and fragmentation of content into tidy teaching units, such a holistic approach is not particularly welcomed by those who hold the power to institute programs." Several of the respondents believed that it was not only the educational planners who were in opposition to such programs, but it was also the practitioners, their colleagues. They wrote of their "traditional" peers who were "threatened with change and uncomfortable writing with kids." These colleagues pressured them to do things like "devote at least one quarter to formal grammar" and select a new "standard grammar text with drill exercises." Some writing project graduates carried on knowing that "sometimes I'm a thorn in the sides of . . . [my colleagues] because I don't diagram sentences or work formal grammar."

Teachers' old habits and mixed feelings about new ones were also causing problems for them. As Lisa said, "After sixteen years of teaching, giving up my agendas has been rough." Again, grammar and "correctness" were an issue. "I still have mixed feelings about the lack of emphasis on 'correct' papers," confessed Sheila, who took the project five years earlier. She worried about her students doing poorly on standardized tests like the ACT. Others agreed. "I have had difficulty overcoming the *feeling* that the English curriculum needs to address the traditional grammar issues in traditional ways," explained Terri. Even when teachers saw their students clean up their mechanical errors in later drafts, they still had "difficulty in ignoring the mechanics" in earlier drafts. Some struggled to find ways to "teach required grammar through writing." Others chose to confront the situation directly. "With college-bound seniors I *must* emphasize the correctness over creativity," Sharon asserted. "I am very severe with them concerning mechanical errors, especially run-ons, fragments, and spelling errors." Sam saw it as "a disservice to students to not point out these errors. For many, if they don't get them marked in high school, they never will even know they are misusing the language."

Teachers' Reports of Present Practices

One of the most common changes in teachers' practices, as they reported those changes, was in the area of student choice. LuAnn explained:

> I try to make it more student-centered. . . . Before the project it was almost completely teacher-centered, 'cause that is what I grew up with. . . . That's been one of the major changes. Students have far more choice—even on a bad day, they have more choice than they would have had before I had the project.

Allowing for more student choice often involved a "surrendering of control," or, as Robin said, "letting go and really letting the kids do their thing . . ., letting them have input into their own writing class." Matt said that "the most visible change" in his classroom was that "we talk a lot more about things that aren't necessarily related to the lesson, and I share my writing with them." Lisa, too, had surrendered some control over the agenda in her classroom. She explained what it often looks like now:

> It's noisy in there. It's organized chaos. There are kids conferencing together. I'm conferencing with them. Or sometimes it's stone quiet and everybody's writing. There's such a variety of activities going on; it's no longer the military camp it used to be.

These teachers seemed especially eager to surrender control and allow for more student choice in the area of writing topics. While such an eagerness can in part be explained by the teachers' beliefs that students "need to write about something they know about," Louise offered another explanation:

> I don't like the responsibility of having to be told that this is a good topic or a bad topic. Why let that be in my lap? They have problems writing about a certain topic, I can come back them . . . "Well, you picked it."

Many of the teachers spoke of how they used to co. ly try to come up with writing topics, and then would get "mad the kids for not liking" their ideas.

These teachers also seemed willing to surrender control over what writing they see, but not over when they see writing. Many initially gave up control over due dates, but then reclaimed it. Laura said, "I couldn't keep up." Susan found herself taking home as many as seventy papers a night and without "any sanity by the next day or any time for my own family." While most of the teachers reported that they'd like to give their students more freedom here, just as they were given such freedom in the writing project, all agreed that it was impossible to do so and maintain a level of "sanity."

These teachers also reported that occasionally they do assign "formal papers," often more formulaic than the other writing they attempt to promote. Such assignments are often more likely to be given in regards to literature. Matt explained what he does:

> I have them do an expository paper, a definition is what it is, to define and illustrate the three types of irony. . . . We talk through it step by step. We write the beginning together, then they can devise the supporting paragraphs and do what they want. That's as close to the traditional essay as I get, and it seems to me that's pretty close.

Matt gives his students a framework for this assigned writing—a set of steps—that places it close to the traditional essay. Louise said she does the same when she asks her students to write a "character sketch." Joan, too, spoke of steps when she talked about the "knowledge paragraphs" that she has her students write, and even when she spoke in general about teaching writing as a process: "I teach it. I say writing is a process, and then I teach them the steps." Joan seems to have translated the characteristics of a writing process into a set of prescriptive steps, something that Matt said he fears happens too often: "I'm afraid the writing process has become too rigid in some people's minds."

The teachers also spoke of what it is they were doing with their students' writing. They mentioned both teacher and peer response. Hal explained his own practices in this area:

> Every paper is returned the day after it is written—with rare exceptions. . . . I comment much more. I spend more time with some of these. Before I would write "very good" or "not bad" at the top. Now I give more in-depth comments.

Previously, Hal had mentioned that before the project it was not uncommon for him to avoid reading his students' writing by tossing it in the wastebasket. Now, he generally reads, responds to, and returns their papers within a day. While not all of these teachers were as prompt as Hal, all agreed that in-depth and positive comments are important. Louise explained the nature of the response she gives and encourages her students to give:

> I'm much more conscious about the clarity of their ideas and their strengths. Strength response is something that I think I've put into more effect. From myself as well as peer response. I have them focus on what they like about the paper. Maybe that's the only response I'll do that day.

While all of the teachers agreed that peer response was valuable in their involvement in the writing project, many have tried to implement this practice in their classrooms and have since retreated somewhat. Here, as with the survey respondents, they spoke of their frustration with the superficial nature of their students' responses to one another's writing. In addition, Sheila acknowledged that she was afraid to use peer response. "Part of it is my fear that they will laugh at one another," she said. "And I think it's my own fragile ego, too." Hal said, "I don't get the cooperation from the kids that I really need to do it." Many of the teachers found that their older students were unwilling or reluctant to share their work with their peers. Sheila believed, "They're afraid of hurting each other's feelings. They're so concerned with what this person or that person thinks of them as an individual." As a result, many of these teachers were using peer response less than they had hoped. Hal, however, was still struggling to incorporate it in his classroom. He focused on training the kids to use it, a process that he acknowledged takes a long time:

> Before I'll start peer response I'll have to really create this atmosphere in the classroom that we are not going to be critical of one another. We are not going to have any put-downs, and we are going to put something of substance on the paper, not just "this was good" or "I like this." And it takes me a long time to train the kids to know how to do that. What they wind up doing is mimicking me for a while, which is OK.

Even if he successfully trains his students to respond to one another's writing, Hal and the others are still forced eventually to respond to their students' efforts by giving them a letter grade. Many of the teachers spoke of trying to grade as infrequently as possible and involving the students in some way when they're finally forced to grade. Robin "usually require[s] something like two graded papers in a nine-week period." She allowed her students to "choose what they want to turn in for a grade." Wilma doesn't grade writing "except at the end of the quarter when I have them choose something out of the writing folder that they have revised that they would like to hand in." And most agreed with LuAnn when she said that when she did grade, she graded "more on feeling, content, willingness to share—the risks taken."

It is difficult to envision these teachers' classrooms from their brief self-reports. It does seem that many have moved toward a surrendering of control in their classrooms, accepting a certain level of "organized chaos" and allowing for more student choice. While giving their students some reign with topic choice, these teachers have reserved due dates as their own domain, and occasionally assign writing that leans "close to the traditional essay." Some seem to have codified writing stages into prescribed steps. They make use of positive, in-depth response to their students' writing and struggle to implement peer response. Most delay grading as long as the system will allow them to do so, permitting the students to select those papers that will receive a letter grade.

The case studies will present us with a more vivid and detailed portrait of some of these teachers' practices, but before moving on, I want to explore their responses to one final question: "How do you know that what you're doing now is better than what you did before?"

Teacher Evaluation of Present Practices

These teachers were, for the most part, pleased with the changes in their classroom practices and believed that their post-project practices were better than their pre-project practices. Most also agreed with Rob when he said, "I don't know how I can document that, but I know that's true." When pressed for evidence to support such an evaluation, they most often cited changes in their own attitudes, in their students' attitudes, and in the quantity and quality of student writing. Linda believed that she was "more confident" with herself. Betty said, "I feel better about it, . . . and I like what I'm doing." Sheila went even further: "It's simply more fun to teach literature . . . and writing."

Betty believed that the students were also "having more fun." "The kids are more willing to write"; "they're eager." LuAnn spoke of "the spontaneity":

> I have had many pages from kids who've just brought me a poem or "Here, Mrs. Birch, read this." And then they'll put it on my desk or just hand it to me, and it's not for any particular reason. . . . This never occurred before.

And Marty claimed:

> There is more interest. There are kids who are upset that we don't have a school newspaper. Kids come in with writing, kids you don't have, and that never used to happen. I just think there's more of an interest.

LuAnn and Marty looked to certain student behaviors for support for their belief that their current practices were better than their previous practices. LuAnn spoke of students who turn in nonrequested writing; Marty mentioned the student talk about the lack of a school newspaper. Evidence for Laura was in a different kind of student behavior. She finds it in the look of concentration on her students' faces and the

> Complete silence. Kids are lost in their thoughts—don't want to talk. When twenty kids are in my room and I don't have to say, "OK, now, quiet down." They're doing something they want to do. Or when other kids—somebody is getting a little restless or something, somebody else looks up like, "Quiet down. I'm in the middle of a good thought here."

Hal was pleased that many of his students were writing more than his minimum requirement. He pointed to his students' writing folders as evidence that things had improved:

> One, the quantity of writing that's in there; the fact that most kids are going to have at least thirty-six papers in their folders, whereas before if we had eight to ten pieces of writing a year, that was something. Also when you look through the folders I think you're going to find that each kid will have a variety of types of writing. Even though I've not assigned poetry, I think almost every kid will have a poem. Even though I have not assigned an essay, I think each kid will have an essay. And they do tend to write in various styles. And I think you also will find that even though I haven't given the length requirements, that you will find in every folder at least one clearly lengthy piece of writing—a good-size story the kid has written. . . . And I think if you look at that last nine weeks, you will also find a lot cleaner writing as far as punctuation and all that type of stuff. I think you can spot spelling improvement through the person's folder. And that's the average folder. You've got kids who are not going to be doing that, and you've got kids who've got a lot more than that. . . .

In his students' accumulated writing, Hal saw quantity, variety, length, and improvement as important signs that his post-project practices were an improvement over his past efforts to teach writing. Hal found that his students were writing more, and in spite of the fact that he no longer assigned specific types of writing or certain lengths, his students seemed to write—over the course of a year—a variety of types and lengths. In addition, Hal also found that his students' writing improved in terms of spelling, punctuation, "and all that type of stuff." Kate also looked to the writing her students were doing as support for her practices:

> Some of the pieces of writing are products that I don't think I could ever give an assignment to come up with. I see that as a real valid point for what I'm doing. I could not have said, "Write this," and

that would have been the product. The students came up with it on
their own, and I see that as real positive evidence that what I'm
doing is right. . . . I think they've gone beyond my expectations of
them. I don't think my expectations are too low. I just think that
some of the things they have done they have created because of
their own ideas and willingness to do it.

Kate, like Hal, found that in surrendering some of her control,
her students had gone beyond her past expectations of them. And
Matt was impressed by his students' abilities to talk about their writing. They can talk about where their ideas came from and "what they
think about as they write," he said. "I'm not sure they used to do
that." Matt also said:

I'm not sure I'm confident about what I do. But I finally have
something—I don't mean to sound evangelistic—but I finally have
something that I can believe in. It matches my own philosophy as a
person. . . . I'd say my teaching has probably improved 100 percent.
Just because I've come to understand why I do what I do. Not just
what do I have to do today, but why should it be done this way. . . . .

Matt returned to himself and how he felt as evidence that his
post-writing project practices were better than his previous practices.
For him, evidence was in the fit he felt between his personal philosophy and the belief system promoted by the writing project. His
experience in the writing project had also given him an understanding of why he was doing what he was doing, a rationale that prompts
and supports his practice. His practice now reflected beliefs that had
been made more explicit, and this allowed Matt, like Rob earlier, to
rest more comfortably.

These twenty teachers, like the questionnaire respondents,
believed that their present practices were better than their pre-
project efforts at teaching writing. They offered as support for such
an evaluation the positive changes they noted in their own attitudes,
in their students' attitudes and abilities, and in the quantity, quality,
and variety of their students' writing. Such evidence assured them
that what they were doing now in terms of teaching writing was better than what they did before they went to the writing project.

Chapter Four

Teachers Talk About Their Teaching: Interpretations

I learned, then, from the questionnaires, that these teachers believed their teaching had been greatly changed as a result of their participation in the Iowa Writing Project and that they valued highly such changes. From the interviews, I learned that this change process often began during the workshop and was often perceived as dramatic, sometimes even traumatic. Marilee identified three steps in her change process that resonated with those mentioned by other project graduates: resistance, conversion, and continued uncertainty.

When the teachers I interviewed spoke of the writing project as a facilitator of their change, they seldom mentioned the research they had read; rather, they mentioned "friendship," "camaraderie," "caring," and "closeness." They also spoke of religious conversion, which is not surprising, given that they perceived this change as a surrendering of an old life, a shaking loose from the past, and an acquisition of "a new shape, a new vision," and a new "community." Innovations are acts of faith, and it would seem that because these teachers came to the writing project of their own volition and with a perceived need, and because of the community, catharsis, and success they felt as students in the writing project, particularly in the afternoon workshops, they could more easily hold such faith.

Their talk of community, conversion, and religion helped me understand my own initial aversive response to the writing project graduates I had first met years earlier—Jerie, Sandra, Lin, and Tom—and my sense that there was something cult-like about them. While this "sense of euphoria" and "new birth" may make outsiders—and some insiders—skeptical, these feelings are genuine and may play an essential role in helping propel graduates of the project back into their own classrooms and contexts with the strength, energy, and conviction necessary for change making.

The teachers also indicated that the change process—for most of them—continued after the workshop. Their beliefs evolved, and as they reported those beliefs, they were, for the most part, consonant with those that are central to the writing project and with those reported by the larger body of questionnaire respondents. Such an evolution of belief seems to have moved many of these teachers—as had been true in my own experience—away from the traditional paradigm of writing and writing instruction, the paradigm in which many of us were schooled and had been schooling others.

The writing project, then, does seem to effect change in its graduates, most clearly in their articulated beliefs. Problems arise, however, when we turn to their practices. Many of the teachers I interviewed left the writing project excited about an approach, then they were immediately confronted with the initial struggle of translating such an approach from one context to another. They moved back into classrooms where the school day had not changed and where their problem was not only one of translation—making sense of new concepts in old contexts—but also one of maintaining, as LuAnn said, the "necessary strength and enthusiasm" to carry out those new concepts.

Dissonance: Beliefs and Practices

Obstacles to the implementation of new beliefs, or "things [that] rub up against the concept of the project" as LuAnn referred to them, often created a dissonance between new beliefs and practices. Many spoke to me of their writing project experience as "utopia" and said that "out there in the trenches it just isn't like that." Some, like Hal, believed "education is a highly negative experience" and the teacher must struggle to "twist that around." Eileen struggled to establish the "healthy type of learning environment" that she found in the writing project, while "living in an opposite type of environment." "You're trying to accomplish one thing," she said, "and you're really having to fend off the opposite element all the time." Marty explained the difference he saw between the "ideal" and the "classroom":

> It's more ideal up in my head than it is actually in the classroom. I guess like anybody I'm easily discouraged, so when I come across problems, whether it's a paper load or whether the kid's getting it or something, you know, my human frailty shows. . . . They teach you the philosophy and you just have to go out there and incorporate that philosophy into your lesson plans. And you know you

can't just drop whatever. You have curriculum guides and you've got your principal giving you, "Oh, you want to try this workbook here for teaching study skills this year?" You were already having a hard time getting everything in before you got that, so that means you've got to drop a short story here and a novel there. There's just so much time anyway. You just can't go in and teach a class like the writing project would unless you have a writing class. And now that I'm going to have one, maybe I'll be able to make it a more domed environment.

Marty said he was "easily discouraged" in his efforts to "incorporate that [writing project] philosophy" in his classes. He cited the paper load, curriculum guides, students, administrators, and time as his greatest obstacles to "getting everything in." His desire for a "domed" or protected environment was consistent with the comments of the questionnaire respondents who said that their attempts at implementing new practices were more successful in classes that were devoted to writing as opposed to those that had a broader language arts focus. Perhaps that explained some of the success and satisfaction I felt in my own classroom after my writing project experience. Our curriculum at Tipton High provided separate courses for writing and literature; my assignment in composition may have given me the "domed environment" that Marty sought.

In addition, the teachers identified a variety of factors that they perceived as impediments to the kind of teaching they believed they should be doing. They talked about curricular restraints, a lack of support services, too little room, outsider expectations that good grammar instruction results in good writing, schools and communities that value standardized test scores, their own fears, and an awareness that their students may encounter future high school and college instructors who will expect certain skills and forms to have been mastered. Many were aware of the dissonance that their contexts created between their new beliefs and their practices. Louise, a six-year veteran of teaching, explained the dissonance she saw in her own classroom:

Well, realistically, . . . the workshop idea—the theory I have in my head is not being practiced. Especially with my seventh graders. Conferencing and working very individually with my kids is not being done to the extent I would like to. It's more on a volunteer basis. I do have some kids coming to me and wanting me to talk about their paper . . . but I don't do that with all the kids. Part of that is because when I start working up here with these guys I got the jokers back there who are off in another world. So what I'm doing is monitoring the whole group—keeping everybody on task. . . . Probably one of the most difficult things with me is dealing with the grading—

surrendering the objective tasks of grading—the quizzes and the things where it's easy to say this is the wrong answer. . . . I want to be able to say, "Well, you missed five, so that's this grade." You can't do that with their writing.

It was in part Louise's knowledge of her students that created some dissonance for her. It was also probably Louise's need or felt responsibility for maintaining an orderly room where all students are overtly on task that kept her from practicing what she said she believed. Matt—who had taken all three levels of the project, recently repeated Level I, and taught the project himself—explained this problem:

. . . [T]he writing process in its purest form isn't the way to conduct a classroom, at least not for me. . . . There are kids who don't love writing; there are kids who are in school because they have to be. And even though I think the writing process is wonderful, they don't necessarily share that enthusiasm. So that what they perceive as a lack of structure, they start to take advantage of. . . . [And] I think probably the classroom environment, the noise level, is a hard control to relinquish. Because I know there are several teachers, and I tend to be one, that associate a high noise level with a lack of productivity.

Matt pointed out that his students are well-schooled. They have come to expect a certain kind and level of structure within class-rooms, and when that is absent, even though it might have been replaced by a different sort of structure, they assume that there is none and begin to operate as though that were true. Teachers, too, are well-schooled; they often equate the level of quietness in a class-room with a level of productivity, and therefore find it difficult to relinquish the control they could exercise over noise level.

Sheila, Matt's colleague, was typically more blunt: "We like to be in control," she said. "We're bossy people. We wouldn't be teachers if we weren't."

Louise raised another issue that was an obstacle cited by many teachers in their attempts at moving from belief to practice: evalua-tion. Schools expect teachers to be evaluators. If she must play that role, Louise would rather do it objectively, but she doesn't believe it's possible. In an attempt at solving her dilemma with both control and evaluation, Louise pulled out her grammar book. "And I wasn't going to do that," she said. It made her uncomfortable—put her in conflict with her stated beliefs—but she saw this as the lesser evil.

Sheila's problem with evaluation was different. She said:

Although I hated grading papers in the old days when we circled every error and all that, I still find it very hard not to do it. Even after five years, I still find it hard not to do it. I just think it's ingrained in the English teacher's bloodstream.

Although Sheila believed that circling errors was counterproductive to the development of her students as writers, she was finding it hard to "kick the habit." Sometimes she gave in to the urge. Other times she attempted to satisfy it with other behaviors, like focusing on only one kind of error or writing a suggestion at the end of the paper such as: "Maybe you ought to look at sentence structure; you write a lot of run-on sentences." While these behaviors eased her need, she worried about their effect and acknowledged that "No one has ever come to me and said, 'Help me not write run-on sentences anymore.'"

Wilma, too, was aware of some of the dissonance in her own practice. She explained:

I use textbooks. That doesn't match up with what I believe, but . . . I am torn. I don't like to teach grammar. I teach usage. Actually I really believe that if you sat down and had a total picture of reading and writing, I don't think you even need usage. But I teach it. . . . It's easier for me to teach it that way than it is for me to pool some papers and say, "OK, there are seven people that are misusing the rule of agreement of subject and verb." Theoretically, I believe I should just teach that rule to those seven, but instead I'll teach it to the whole class. Because it's easier for me to do it that way. It's less sitting down looking through the papers making charts. It's less paperwork. It's less time. So it doesn't match there because I believe one thing, and I do another. I believe that everybody should be workshopped. And I never get the time because of the way the curriculum is set up. There's very little time to incorporate all that has to be done—that I believe should be done—and get all of the rest of the stuff in that needs to be gotten in in ninth-grade language arts— reading, writing, listening, speaking. So it doesn't match up there. . . . I try to do a little bit of mixing. It's almost like a crisscross or herringbone effect. I do a little bit of this, then I do a little bit of my thing. Hopefully it comes together. I don't know if it does.

Sheila, aware that some of her students want "guided and directed assignments," was doing a similar kind of mixing.

I figure that way everybody is within their comfort zone part of the time at least. If they don't feel really comfortable with free reign, then they can be more comfortable when there is more directed assignment, and vice versa.

Wilma and Sheila, rather than abandon old practices and replace them with new ones, seem to have created a contradictory patchwork quilt of old and new. Hal, too, spoke of engaging in old practices along

with his new ones. He claimed that he did not value these old practices, but he used them to "satisfy administration and parents." Wilma
seems to do this mixing to satisfy curriculum requirements; Sheila
said she was doing this to satisfy some of her students.

Karla finds that 10 to 20 percent of her students "want to carry
home the grammar book . . . and do the drills and diagramming."
Although Karla sees such work as pointless—she called it "monas-
tery work"—she'll sometimes give in to these students' desires, often
negotiating with them. She believes that these students value such
work because "that's what school means."

Many of the teachers believed that something quite different
from their own notions of sound practice was expected of them. Lisa
illustrated that with a tale from her school:

> We had one administrator [who] was supportive of what we were
> doing but didn't understand it, and the other teacher came up to
> me, and she said, "I've just had my first evaluation."
>   I said, "How'd it go?"
>   "Do you know what she said to me? She watched me do a
> whole writing workshop and it went marvelous. I was conferenc-
> ing; the kids were working. And after the class she said, 'Can I come
> back when you're teaching?' I thought that was what I was doing."

Jake finds some irony in the situation:

> In this age of outcomes-based education, it's strange to see this
> pocket of quiet rebellion against behaviorism. There seems to be a
> struggle. You see a lot of administrators accepting that teachers are
> going to these projects, and they'll pay for a workshop or two. I'm
> not sure they understand the implications or the politics of it. I
> think they really are naive. There's sort of a small revolution going
> on underneath their noses . . . that they're financing.

Such expectations from administrators, parents, students, and
other teachers often push teachers into practices they no longer
value. Generally they are confronted with choices and are aware of
the dissonance that results in their electing to do other than that in
which they believe. Many spoke of feeling guilty or pressured. Wilma
said, "I feel that I'm doing better, but I feel a great amount of pressure, almost more pressure than I've ever had before, because I don't
feel that how I teach is how the public believes I should teach."
Wilma believed that the public would have her be "more dictatorial,
regimented, demanding." She's unwilling to give in to such pressures, she said, because

> I don't feel that's a good atmosphere. I need to try and make these
> students realize that they're in a safe room. That they can write.

They can feel comfortable. I don't believe that you can become better if you are not in a safe zone.

These same pressures and expectations were creating external conflict for LuAnn:

> I don't know if age has much to do with it, but the longer you've taught one way, sometimes it's harder to adjust to the other. And when for thirteen years you've assigned things, you've become comfortable with it. "Write me two hundred words for tomorrow on a story we just read," let's say, and you become comfortable with that and so sometimes it's easy to fall back into the old routines—at least for me it was. You have less conflict that way. . . . [But you have internal conflict] because you feel like your students deserve more than this. Or you know there's another way. I have been exposed to another way of doing it. Before I wasn't. Now I have, and so when I revert back to the old way, then there's conflict. "Well, now this isn't fair to these kids. This isn't the way this should be done." . . . But I can read a good book to help me get over the internal conflict. But the external conflict is there in every memo and school board meeting.

The pressures these teachers feel come indirectly—simply in noticing that their colleagues are not teaching as they are—or directly in "every memo and school board meeting." LuAnn also feels a kind of pressure within herself that is created by years of experience in old practices that had become comfortable routines. Such pressures from within and without to retrieve these old practices, however, are counterbalanced by new and valued knowledge. When she slips into old routines, she feels guilty. Eventually, however, LuAnn could not maintain the balance. She admitted that she had begun to compromise in order to avoid the external pressures.

Dissonance, then, for these teachers is created by internal and external factors. Internally, their own fears, expectations, natures, and past experiences may impede their efforts at implementing or maintaining new practices. Externally, they are confronted with curriculum guides, paper loads, a lack of time and support services, too little room, and a set of roles; all of these are aspects of the contexts into which they've returned, and all play a part in determining how successfully they can practice what they believe. In addition, there are the individuals who people these contexts—the students, administrators, parents, and other teachers—who might directly or indirectly challenge or limit these teachers' efforts at implementation. Again, I was reminded of my own experience: the straight-A students, the basketball coach, the set of angry parents.

The Role of Support

Given this potential for dissonance, support became important to many of the teachers as they attempted to put their new beliefs into practice. They wanted to turn to others who shared their beliefs. "I felt a need for reinforcement," said Laura. "There was another girl in my program, and I've talked to her. Like even at the supermarket maybe for fifteen minutes we'll talk." Matt explained:

> We tend to go back into our classrooms and be solitaire—even though I think the writing project is a great model for professional talk—it seems like that dissipates fairly quickly. We get caught up in our schedules and our routine with all this stuff we have to do, and we don't talk out problems. I think that's probably most of what's missing.

Matt, however, considered himself to be fortunate:

> . . . [T]here were three of us out of four in the English department within the space of two years who had had the writing project, so we had collegial support. And the three rooms were close enough together in the building that when we had a success or a problem, we weren't far away. The farthest we usually had to go was the teachers' lounge, and we could talk there.

Not all of the teachers were so fortunate. Some returned to districts where no other teachers had taken the writing project. Others, like Marty, who was teaching at an urban school where the majority of the large English department had taken the writing project, still found that there was no collegial support. "I don't think there's any two rooms together," he said. "We hardly ever see one another." Laura felt too "swamped" to get together with the five or six other teachers in her small, rural district that had taken the writing project, and she believed her administration preferred it that way: ". . .they don't want the teachers unified. They want them separate so they can control them," she said.

Susan, who was teaching in a rural district in northern Iowa, believed it was not control but cowardice that led her administrators to abandon her and a colleague in their first year of attempting to implement post-project practices:

> When I first came back from the writing project, the reaction was hostile. . . . [The board president's wife] went on such a tirade about the writing and how the fourth-grade teacher and I were teaching that we had to do a public presentation on our writing project. . . . She didn't want journal writing. She's one of these right-wing, anti-humanism type people, and she said the students

had no business writing their thoughts and feelings. That's none of my business and school is no place for that. They should be learning formal writing only. . . .

It was to the point that she was calling me at school and I'd be in class so I'd go down to the office and I would get a message that I was supposed to call Mrs. So-and-So and I would call her and she would go after me. . . . I just defended the program, then she attacked me as being not Christian, and then I would defend myself, then she would get mad and hang up. And her husband went to the school board and said that I was now calling her at home and harassing her. It was one of the most difficult times of my teaching, and I went through it because of the writing project. Here I was doing the best teaching of my life, and I was under attack.

And we came out of it OK, but the point was we went through two months of intimidating treatment, and I guess I was disappointed we were forced out on the block like that because our principal and superintendent thought that was the way to handle it. The superintendent said, "I know you have a good program and you know that you have a good program going, show the community." . . .

The principal said, "Oh, it's not that big a deal. Don't worry about it. You'll be fine." Well, it was a big deal. It was our profession. It was our reputation in a lot of ways, and we did feel a lot of pressure, and he just made it real trivial.

And the husband of the lady that attacked us, the school board president, had a pork producers' meeting or something that night and didn't even show up. . . . And I thought our presentation was excellent. Rose and I worked on it for two months. . . . And this lady at the end got up and read a bunch of things. You know, we had a look-'em-in-the-eye presentation, and she got up and read out of newspaper articles. She hung herself basically. . . . So it's over. But it was a real emotional thing. And I don't think it was fair to the kids. I don't think I taught as well. I was real uptight about that. I was real on guard about everything I said or did.

Some teachers were fortunate enough to move back into contexts where they were able to find collegial support, even if it was only an infrequent fifteen-minute chat in the supermarket with another writing project graduate. Most moved from a new and enthusiastic community back into the relative isolation of their old classrooms. Many of them did not find the collegial support they wanted—due to factors such as busy schedules or the physical layout of their schools. For Susan it was not merely the absence of support for her new practices; it was also the presence of open hostility toward those practices. In spite of the fact that she felt herself to be doing "the best teaching" of her life, Susan found herself under parental attack and with no real support from her administrators.

Other teachers also reported confronting outsider expectations about the nature of good English instruction that contradicted their own newly developed expectations. Such circumstances directed some of these teachers back to the writing project, either to Level II (the two-week workshop) or Level III (the year-long journal-keeping seminar), seeking the support they desired. Karla wanted "a support group," Wilma wanted to get her "hands on those books," and LuAnn needed "some vitamin therapy." Robin believed, "Both Levels II and III just put me further and further into confidence in what I was doing." Hal found it to be a relief "to sit there every two weeks and talk to other people." Often the talk would revolve around guilt or failure, and participants would "pat you on the back and say, 'Hey, don't feel guilty.'"

Many of the teachers also reported engaging in a variety of teaching practices outside the classroom that were directed at building support for their new beliefs and practices. Matt said that whenever he "share[s] a student's writing in class, a copy of it goes home to the parents with a note." This practice has earned him the praise of both administrators and parents and has convinced some parents that their children can and do write well without direct instruction in grammar. A practice that is more common with these teachers is that of teaching the parents about writing during parent-teacher conferences. Several reported using these conferences to explain to parents their approaches to writing instruction and using their students' writing folders as evidence that such approaches were effective.

Lisa, of the twenty teachers I interviewed the only one to be sent to the writing project, seemed to be the most actively involved in attempting to change outsiders' expectations about "good" English instruction and build community support for her teaching. She talked to parents at conferences, and she wrote a column in the local newspaper:

> I've been writing a column for the last three years now, just featuring student writing, and some of them are instructional on things like invented spelling. . . . We'll run several of the first graders' stories with the translations, and we'll just do a little instruction in the column on growing writers and how you'll see these invented spellings and that type of thing. So it's community knowledge that when a paper comes home with misspelled words at the first-grade level, don't panic. It's going to be OK. And showing high school writers taking a piece through three revisions so parents can see what they're doing with that.

Lisa believed that she had garnered some community support by publishing student writing and explaining things like invented spelling and revision. In addition, she had been actively engaging her administrators in dialogue about writing instruction, teacher evaluation, curriculum, and inservice programs. She explained:

> We are in our district into an inservice program of effective schools training, which is Madeline Hunter and things like that. So I've been fighting the battle with them. "How does this cross over here?" I've been telling the superintendent, "I don't think you could walk into one of your elementary teacher's writing workshops and give either a good or bad evaluation because you don't understand what you're looking at." And I think he sent the principal [to the writing project] because of that. . . . Just last year we've been fighting the curriculum battle with him. The first thing he did was hand out scope and sequence charts, and the first thing I said was, "This is not possible. We can't do that . . . under what we're doing now."

Lisa challenged her administrators with following through on the commitment she believed they had made to the writing project and those teachers they had sent to project institutes. With the popular base of support she had earned among parents for the kind of writing instruction she practiced, a firm but polite manner, and a ready supply of alternatives, Lisa seems to have been quite successful in modifying the context in which she and her colleagues struggled to implement their notions of sound writing instruction. Her teaching practices outside the classroom have given her more room to engage in practices inside the classroom that are more consonant with her beliefs about the teaching of writing.

Lisa's experiences reminded me of my own. My colleague, Jerie Weasmer, was committed to building community support for our writing program. She wrote and placed articles in the community newspaper each time we attended professional conferences or one of our students published a piece of writing or won an award or contest. While some of our colleagues saw this as shameless self-promotion, it did seem to build community support. Parents and even school board members stopped us in the grocery store to compliment us on the most recent issue of *Kaleidoscope*, the literary magazine we had begun publishing in order to showcase student writing, or to talk with us about their own adolescent's work. As I mentioned in Chapter One, our principal had attended my writing project institute on visitor's day. Jerie and I occasionally channeled articles on the teaching of writing to him. As a result, he limited enrollments in writing courses to twenty and offered support whenever we were challenged.

Just as it had become important—indeed essential—to me, support became important to many of these teachers; they wanted to

turn to others who shared their beliefs. Some teachers—like me—
were fortunate enough to move back into contexts where they were
able to find some collegial or administrative support. Most, however,
moved from a new and enthusiastic community back into the relative isolation of their old classrooms. Many of them did not find the
collegial support they wanted due to conditions like busy schedules
or the physical layout of their schools. Many also reported confronting outside expectations—from other teachers, administrators, and
community members—about the nature of good English instruction
that contradicted their own newly developed expectations. Such circumstances directed some of these teachers back to the writing
project, seeking the support they desired.

Practices

It is difficult to envision these teachers' classrooms from their brief
self-reports. It does seem that many have moved toward a surrendering of control in their classrooms, accepting a certain level of "organized chaos" and allowing for more student choice, particularly with
writing topics. The teachers have, however, reserved due dates as
their own domain, and occasionally they assign writing that leans
"close to the traditional essay." Some even seem to have codified
writing stages into prescribed steps. They also make use of positive,
in-depth response to their students' writing and struggle to implement peer response. Most delay grading as long as the system will
allow them to do so, permitting the students to select those papers
that will receive a letter grade. In addition, several teachers engage in
practices outside their classrooms in an attempt to change some of
those "things [that] rub up against the concept of the project."

As they wrote and spoke of their beliefs and practices, the most
common area of dissent or dissonance involved the importance of
"correctness" in student writing. This is where teachers often felt
they were believing or operating in opposition to writing project
principles. Just how much effort should a writing teacher devote to
spelling, punctuation, syntax, and form? And what shape should
this effort take?

Why should this be the sticking point for so many teachers?
Richard Young's (1978, 31) description of the more traditional paradigm of writing instruction provides some clues:

> The overt features . . . are obvious enough: the emphasis on the
> composed product rather than the composing process; the analysis

of discourse into words, sentences, and paragraphs; the classification of discourse into description, narration, exposition, and argument; the strong concern with usage (syntax, spelling, punctuation) and with style (economy, clarity, emphasis); the preoccupation with the informal essay and the research paper; and so on.

A preoccupation with correctness, then, is central to the more traditional paradigm of writing instruction. These teachers were well-schooled in this paradigm; it was a fundamental element of the writing instruction they had received, and—for many of them—fundamental to the instruction they had been providing their own students for years. Given its central role in the traditional paradigm and their histories as students and teachers, it is not surprising that it should appear as a common area of dissent or dissonance.

I had been given a clearer picture of writing project graduates and of their perceived change processes, contexts, beliefs, and practices. Such a picture suggests that these teachers have indeed been influenced by their participation in the writing project, particularly at the level of their stated beliefs. It is in the area of their practices where we begin to see more dissonance, and so it is to their practices that we now turn. The case studies of four of these teachers—presented in the next two chapters—will offer a more vivid and detailed portrait of these writing project graduates' classroom practices.

Chapter Five

Four Teachers Teaching: Successes

From the group of twenty teachers I had interviewed, I selected four for case studies and classroom observations. As the methodology section in the Appendix explains in greater detail, I sought teachers whose teaching contexts had changed the least since the years immediately preceding their involvement in the Project, whose schools were located within sixty miles of my home base in eastern Iowa, and who most expressed an interest in the questions raised by the study and a willingness to work with me in answering those questions. In addition, I was able to select four teachers whose teaching assignments had them working at the ninth grade, thus providing the study with a tighter focus. (See Table 1 for a complete profile of these teachers.)

I used these case studies in an attempt to paint greater detail into my emerging portrait of writing project graduates and their post-project lives. After reviewing these four teachers and their contexts, this chapter will examine some of what I learned from them and their students as I spent a semester in their classrooms.

The Teachers and Their Contexts

Robin

Robin Barnes, then thirty-two, had taught for four years at the time of her first writing project institute where we became classmates. At the time of this study, she was in her tenth year of teaching. Robin, since that first institute, had gone on to participate in both Levels II and III of the writing project. She had a bachelor's degree in English and journalism.

Table 1
Participant Profile: Case Study Teachers

Name	Age	School Name	Grades	Town (and size)	District (and size)	Exper pre-wp[1]	Exper pre-cs[2]	IWP Levels	Grades Taught	Classes
Robin	32	North Lincoln H.S.	9-12	rural	North Lincoln (800)	4	9	I, II, III	9-12	3 x English 1 2 x Creative Writing 1 x Journalism 1 x Publications
Wilma	39	Wolburn H.S.	9-12	Wolburn (5040)	Wolburn (1400)	9	14	I, II	9-12	5 x Language Arts 1 1 x Journalism
Eileen	30	Exeter Mills J/S. H.S.	7-12	Exeter Mills (600)	Exeter Mills (200)	4	6	I, III	7, 9-12	1 x English I 1 x EnglishII 1 x English IV 1 x Drama 1 x 7th Reading
Hal	41	Stone Creek J.H.S.	7-9	Swansen (1860)	Stone Creek (1100)	16	18	I, II, III	8-9	4 x 9th LanguageArts 1 x 9th French 1 x Exploratory French

[1] *Exper pre-wp*: Years of teaching experience prior to involvement in the writing project.

[2] *Exper pre-cs*: Years of teaching experience prior to involvement in the case study.

Robin was teaching at North Lincoln High School. Her school is a long, flat, brick building that was constructed in the middle of a cornfield when several small, rural communities united to form the North Lincoln District with eight hundred students. Robin had a good working relationship with her administrators and had found them to be amiable, interested, and verbally supportive of her efforts to improve writing instruction.

Robin's course schedule included one section of Publications, one of Journalism, two of Creative Writing, and three sections of English I. This last course, for ninth graders, was a four-quarter class. The first two quarters were devoted to study skills on Mondays through Thursdays; Fridays were set aside for writing. Every two weeks a paper was due for peer workshopping; on alternate Fridays students did "writing clean-up." In addition, the class wrote in their journals for five to ten minutes each day. In the third quarter of this course, Robin moved into full-time, student-directed reading and writing workshops.

Robin asked that I work with her second period English I section, believing them to be "more attentive and cooperative" and "more in tune with" what she said about response than were her other two sections. There were seventeen students of mixed abilities in this section—eight boys and nine girls.

Wilma

Wilma Marshak, then thirty-nine, was teaching at Wolburn High School. Prior to her first writing project institute where we, too, became classmates, Wilma had taught for nine years. At the time of this study she was in her fourteenth year of teaching. Wilma has a bachelor's degree in English and had taken several graduate courses in journalism and writing, including Level II of the writing project.

The Wolburn Community School District had fourteen hundred students in grades kindergarten through twelve and is located in a county seat community of just over five thousand residents. The high school, a large, older, three-story brick building sits on a tree-lined street at the edge of Wolburn. Wilma reported that she spoke with her principal often about writing and that she had found him to be curious about and supportive of her efforts to improve writing instruction. Recently he and the superintendent had named her chairperson of the district's K–12 language arts program.

Wilma's course schedule included one section of Journalism and five of Language Arts I. This last course, for ninth graders and lasting for four quarters, was "always changing," and had "no rigid curriculum." Instead, Wilma said she taught what she wanted for as long as she wanted. In the fall Wilma began with a library skills unit because "I answer too many questions when we go to the library for research." She then moved into a writing unit and finally into a literature unit to complete the first two quarters of the year. Each day the class spent five to ten minutes writing in their response logs.

Wilma selected her sixth-period Language Arts I section for this study because it was a class full of "gifted" and "neat writers" who were "willing to share" and "get involved in anything." There were eighteen students of mixed abilities in this section, evenly divided between girls and boys.

Eileen

Eileen Bauman, then thirty, had taught for four years prior to taking Level I of the writing project; at the time of the study she was in her sixth year of teaching. Eileen had earned a bachelor's degree in English and had also taken Level III of the writing project. I first met Eileen when I interviewed her for this study at her rural farm home a few miles north of Tipton, my former school district and home.

Eileen was teaching junior and senior high school in rural and impoverished Exeter Mills, population six hundred. The Exeter Mills Consolidated School District, with only two hundred students, is one of the state's smallest and poorest districts, but it had stubbornly refused to join with any of the neighboring schools that had made advances toward reconsolidation. The small, two-story, brick building sits on a rise in the middle of town where it was constructed near the turn of the century. Eileen's principal, she believed, was basically uninterested in what was happening in her classroom. She felt he was "mean" and created a "negative atmosphere" in the school. He was fond of commenting loudly that none of his current students or teachers were any good.

Eileen's class schedule included one section each of English I, English II, English IV, Drama, and seventh-grade Reading. The English I course, for ninth graders, had no set curriculum and changed from year to year. In the fall Eileen began the course with a six-week "Writers' Workshop Unit" before moving on to a "Western Unit" and then a "Problem-Solving Unit." Each day the students and Eileen spent five to ten minutes writing in their logs. There were fourteen students in this mixed-ability class, only three of whom were female.

Hal

Prior to taking the first level of the writing project, Hal Thompson had taught for sixteen years; at the time of the study he was in his eighteenth year of teaching. I first met Hal when I interviewed him

in his living room for this study. His wife, also a teacher, was participating in her first writing project that summer. She sat silently with
us, not participating but attentive to my questions and Hal's
responses. Hal, like Robin, had taken all three levels of the writing
project. He has a bachelor's degree in French and has done graduate
coursework in English.

Hal, then forty-one, was teaching at Stone Creek Junior High.
The Stone Creek Community School District had eleven hundred
students in kindergarten through twelfth grade and one high school,
one junior high, and three elementary schools located in three different communities. The junior high is a low, modern, blond brick
building with few windows. It sits alone on the east edge of
Swansen, population 1,860. Hal seemed to have a good working relationship with his administrators. His principal was interested, supportive, and enthusiastic about Hal's efforts to improve writing
instruction and had made Hal director of the school's first-thing-in-
the-morning Sustained Silent Reading and Writing (SSRW) Program.
As director, Hal had conducted several writing workshops for his
colleagues and administrators, getting them to think about their own
writing and showing them how they could respond to their students'
writing and encourage peer response.

Hal's class schedule included one section each of Exploratory
French and ninth-grade French, and four sections of ninth-grade Language Arts. This last course included studies in "reading, writing,
speaking, listening, spelling, vocabulary, grammar, and usage skills,"
but Hal made it clear that "the emphasis in this class will be on
writing." Students were graded in four areas: "the writing basket;
journal writing; book reports; and vocabulary, spelling, usage, and
grammar." For their writing basket grade, students merely needed to
turn in approximately one piece per week. Hal informed his students
that

> almost anything in almost any style or form [is acceptable]. You
> may write stories or parts of stories, personal opinions, poems,
> plays, or you just may want to "talk" to me on paper about what-
> ever is on your mind. Nearly any topic is acceptable. Your piece
> may be only partially done or it may be totally finished. It may be
> very long or very short or somewhere in between. It may be written
> in pencil or pen or it may be typed. It may have things erased or
> crossed out or it may have arrows showing how it may be rear-
> ranged. You may redo or revise anything you've written and turn it
> in again. Just write something and put it in the basket. As long as
> it's in good taste and demonstrates some thought and effort, you
> will get credit for it. Please turn your writing in on entire sheets of
> paper so I will have plenty of room to make comments.

Every day Hal posted a sign outside his classroom door that announced the activity for that day. Approximately one or two days each week were given to vocabulary, spelling, usage, and grammar; another two days to "free writing and reading"; and one day to "sharing." In addition, the class spent the first five minutes of each period "practicing writing" in their journals.

Hal selected without hesitation his second period section of ninth-grade Language Arts for my observation. "They're more serious and excited," he said. "They're gonna make my day." There were twenty students of mixed abilities in this section—thirteen girls and seven boys. Immediately following this class session, Hal had an open planning period. Given this and Hal's ability to think out loud, it often seemed I received more information about his plans and perceptions than I did about the other three teachers, none of whom had an open period near her target class.

Robin, Wilma, Eileen, and Hal—like the other interviewees and the questionnaire respondents—subscribed to those seven writing project principles. They believed that writing is a complicated process with characteristic features, such as composing, drafting, revising, and editing, and time must be allowed for these features. They believed that writers need to have ownership over their own processes and products, that, as Robin said, "You need to write about what's important to you," and writers need readers to respond to their work—positively. They believed that successful writing results more often from attention to meaning than from adherence to standard conventions of grammar, spelling, and punctuation. They believed, as Hal said, that "the student learns to write by writing," that students and teachers need to write regularly.

Given these beliefs, Robin, Wilma, Eileen, and Hal had attempted to design their instruction accordingly. They strived to create an atmosphere that "make[s] the student want to write." They affirmed their students' efforts by using positive teacher response, then expanded their audience by providing for peer response. Their goal in all this, they reported, was to help their students become "confident writers and responsible, sensitive responders."

These beliefs and intentions are inarguably attractive in the abstract, but it is at the level of implementation that they must be studied, for it is only at that level that specific successes and problems are encountered, and I found myself curious about such specifics. In this chapter I survey successful practices employed by these four, that is, those practices where the results seemed to closely represent the teachers' intentions, and I explore possible reasons for

such successes. In Chapter Six, then, I turn to those practices where
the results seemed problematic.

Successes

Over the course of my visits to the four teachers' classrooms, three
of their practices began to draw my attention; the practices and the
results of those practices seemed to closely represent the teachers'
intentions. All of the teachers used journals; all were involved in
efforts to build support and reshape their teaching contexts; all made
frequent use of positive and specific responses to affirm their students' writings.

Journals

Journal use, one of the most distinctive features of these four classrooms, provided the most popular place and context for frequent
student and teacher writing in the classes I observed. All four teachers asked their students to maintain and write in some form of bound
journals. Eileen called them "logs"; Wilma called them "responding
logs"; Hal and Robin referred to them as "journals." All four generally began each class period with from five to ten minutes of journal
writing time, and all used that time to write in their own journals.

As I observed their classes and read their students' journals, I
noticed that the journals seemed to serve three general purposes:
note taking, response writing, and open writing. In most cases they
were used for open writing, either on an optional topic proffered by
the teacher, or more often, on a topic selected by the student. The
intention here seemed to be simply to "practice writing." Hal
explained this to his students on a handout that he gave the students
on the first day of class:

> The only way to learn to write well is to practice writing. We will
> spend the first five minutes of each class period this year doing just
> that—practicing . . . in a journal. During this five minutes, you may
> write anything which is on your mind. If something good or bad has
> happened, write about it. If you are happy or sad about something,
> write about it. If you are angry, write about it. Write about whatever
> is on your mind, but write for the whole five minutes.

The emphasis in such open journal writing, then, was generally
on personal expressive writing and on developing a sense of fluency—
getting the students to experience the feeling of composing for a solid
five or ten minutes. Eileen, Robin, and Wilma often volunteered

optional topics for such journal writing. One day Robin suggested, "What's something you would really miss if it were taken away from you?"

At other times journals were used for response writing, writing in response to something that was read or done. In such cases the teacher would offer a specific prompt to encourage the students to think about what they had read or done. One day Hal read aloud "The Lady or the Tiger?," a short story by Frank Stockton, and then directed his students: "In your journal answer that question [in the title] and tell why you think that. There is no right answer, but you must try and persuade others. Tell why." Following this journal assignment, the class shared their responses in a discussion of the story.

Wilma, too, used journal writing as a way of getting her students to think and as a precursor to discussion. One day, after a particularly rough class session in the library on using resources there, Wilma directed her students to, "Consider something in your responding logs. Tell me how yesterday's lesson went." She added, "Let's write for ten minutes on that. You're gonna help me and I'm gonna help you by doing this." Everyone wrote for the entire ten minutes. The discussion that followed was animated and interactive, and it seemed to ease the anxiety level that had risen during the previous day's lesson.

In addition, the four teachers sometimes directed their students to think about writing by writing in their journals. Wilma once told her students to "write about what ideas you have about writing." Robin, after a paper exchange with students from another school, directed her students to write in their own journals: "After reading these papers, what things in these writings impressed you? What would you like to improve or try in your own writing after having seen these writings from students in another school?" All such response writing was more teacher-directed than was the open writing the students did in their journals. Generally, the function, audience, and topic of such writing were determined by the teacher.

The third purpose that the journals served in these four classrooms was for note taking. They were seldom used in this way, but occasionally the instructors would direct their students to do something such as "mark the ten [vocabulary] words down in your log" or record notes there while watching a film. Of the three purposes served by journals, note taking was used the least, response writing occurred more frequently, and open writing occurred most every day.

Issues of privacy and evaluation were intertwined in these four classrooms with regard to the journals. Robin and Hal never read their students' journals unless invited to read a specific entry; instead, they simply counted pages at their students' desks in order to "check" the journals. Eileen and Wilma periodically read and responded to their students' journals but gave them the option of writing something such as "do not read" above a particular entry.

Robin explained her policy concerning journal privacy in a handout she gave her students at the beginning of the year:

> Remember that the journals are for you. They need not ever be shared with anyone, and I will never read them unless you want me to. If ever there is something that you would like me to read, mark it and place it in the collection box. Do take precautions to keep your journal in a safe place if you do not want it to be read by anyone.

Believing that the journals were for her students and that they had a right to expect privacy in them, Robin did not read their entries unless invited. She cautioned her students to protect their journals and warned them that their parents or friends might be curious about what they had written. "Parents are real curious about what you think, about what you're writing," she said. Then she assured her students that she believed, "You have a right to your thoughts," and that she would always back such a right. "I really don't have any respect for someone who invades someone else's privacy." Robin ended this caution with a story about the mother of a student of hers who read her son's journal and was concerned about his swearing in it. "I backed him 100 percent, although I'm not delighted by swearing," Robin said.

Hal that year added a new policy that "Anyone caught reading someone else's journal is subject to failure for the quarter." These four teachers' concern for privacy in their students' journals arose from situations where that privacy had been violated and students hurt, as well as from a belief that students need a safe place to write honestly "about things that are important to you . . ., things you're interested in, things that concern you."

Hal began each class session with some brief time for journal writing. His students entered noisily, talking as they dumped their books at their desks, retrieved their journals from the file drawer where they were kept, and took their seats. Quietly, Hal would simply state, "All right, let's write in our journals." The room grew immediately quiet as everyone began writing. Hal generally sat in a student desk, leaning back away from his journal, writing with his left hand. He stared seriously at his paper, pausing to look around the room only when an occasional student grew overtly restless. The three other teachers, too, seldom directed their attention beyond their own journal writing during the time set aside for it. And students in all four classes generally wrote silently, pausing periodically to chew on their pens or tap them on their papers, their eyes staring upward at nothing or glancing sideways at their neighbors, their lips silently mouthing a word or two before they returned to their writing. Hal always closed this open journal writing time with, "All right, finish up whatever thought you're on." Robin prompted her students to quit writing by saying, "I'd like you to find a good stopping point."

The students seemed to take their journal writing just as seriously as their teachers did. They reported, and their journals revealed, that most made use of the time to write about themselves, things that were happening in their lives, their friends, and school. Ken, one of Eileen's students, wrote about his classes in the second entry of his log:

> Today is the second day of school. I wish I would have thought of something previously today. I'll do that tomorrow. This year has been a lot different from last year. We have all three of the new teachers. It seems like we don't even see the junior high kids anymore, but I guess that's because we have all these different classes. I like "Spanish" and I think it will be fun to learn a new language. Of course I like "English" a lot too. "Earth Science" is what we have fifth hour. I'm sure it'll be much more interesting than "Physical Science" was last year. A lot of the terms aren't brand new like everything was in Physical Science last year.

In this early entry, Ken was still struggling to find his "journal voice." In general, much of their writing here tended to be personal expressive, and sometimes it led to longer pieces that were shared with their peers or teachers. Tammy, another of Eileen's students, explained what she did in her log:

> I don't write fiction. I write about what I think is going on now. If I watch a movie and I like a part of it, I could write it down and then make a story out of that part. In my murder story it happened like that. I watched *Friday the 13th*. I began that [murder story] in my log.

Occasionally the teachers directed or encouraged their students to read their own journals. Hal told his students they should do this because: "You have taken the time to write it. You may find it humorous. You may also find ideas in your journal for a piece for the writing basket. It's a good source of ideas." Wilma told her students that reading through their journals might "trigger something" to write about.

All four teachers, then, used journals in similar ways and with similar intentions. Primarily, these journals became a "safe" place to "practice writing" regularly, a place for the students and teachers to express their thoughts and write about their lives. Secondarily, the journals became a place to think about something that had happened in class, a place for the students and teachers to respond to the teachers' direct prompts to do such thinking. Such use put the teachers more directly in control of the journal writing; function, audience, and topic were usually all determined by the teachers. The prompts here often required the students to write about literature or writing.

Finally, the journals infrequently became a place to record things such as vocabulary words or notes from a lesson. This purpose was the most limiting and the most limited of the three. In general, the four teachers and their students seemed to take seriously their opportunities to write in their journals where they often sowed the seeds of longer pieces, which were later shared with their classes.

The journals as used, then, would seem to have been consonant with the teachers' intentions and with several of the writing project principles: They generally provided for regularity of writing for both students and teachers and allowed for student ownership over topics, permitting the students to draw on their own experiences. When prompts were given, the journals provided another context and purpose for writing.

Building Support

One set of teaching practices discussed earlier that falls outside standard in-class practices yet was obvious with these four teachers included efforts to build support. Here the teachers seemed to be attempting to inform the people in their schools and communities, thereby altering their teaching contexts so that their classroom practices could more nearly reflect their new beliefs and intentions.

Although Eileen had found her efforts to be less than satisfactory given the negativity of her principal, all four teachers reported talking frequently with their administrators about the teaching of writing, not just at their own grade levels and subject areas, but across the curriculum and through the grades. "We can't only do it in the English department. It's got to be district-wide and K–12," Wilma had repeatedly told her administrators. And as I mentioned earlier, Wilma's administrators seemed to be listening; she had recently been named chairperson of the district's K–12 language arts program.

Hal, too, had been lobbying his administrators for support for "process instruction" in writing. As director of the school's Sustained Silent Reading and Writing (SSRW) Program, Hal had conducted formal and informal writing workshops for his colleagues and administrators, getting them to write, think about their own writing, respond to one another's writing, and showing them how they could respond to their students' writing and encourage peer response. Teachers often stopped him in the hall or lounge with questions about writing or to share a piece written by a student. Hal believed that his own students in recent years had become more receptive to writing because they were operating in a school where it had come to be expected.

All four of the teachers spent time talking with their colleagues about writing and sharing their students' work, sometimes in an effort to encourage these other teachers to take the writing project. Mary Lou, a speech teacher and colleague of Robin's, commented, "She's been indoctrinating us with this good writing stuff. There are a few of us now who support one another with writing and reading." The talk with colleagues is reminiscent of "singing the praises of the project" and the desire to be "crusaders," which the other teachers reported earlier. It is, then, a kind of proselytizing.

The teachers' intention, again, seemed to be to build support and alter their contexts so that their classroom practices could more nearly reflect their beliefs and objectives. It is difficult to assess the extent to which their lobbying efforts were successful in that sense, but it seemed clear that those who peopled their contexts believed that there was greater local awareness of "process instruction" than there had been prior to their "indoctrination." Talking with colleagues and administrators as Robin, Wilma, Eileen, and Hal did, in some sense, then, altered their environments and built support for their writing instruction.

Teacher Response

"Writers of all ages need readers to respond to their work at various stages," begins the fifth of the seven writing project principles. All four of these teachers agreed and provided for various forms of response to the work that their students wrote. The purpose of such response, these teachers told their students, was "to get you to write" and to "help you build on your strengths." This response fell into two general categories: teacher response and peer response.

Given that the function of response was to encourage and affirm, all of these teachers spoke of such response as being "positive"; this is also consonant with the fifth writing project principle. The teachers believed that their students had experienced little or no "positive" response to their writing, so they typically made an event of introducing it to their students very near the beginning of the year. Eileen, because she had taught all of her ninth graders in junior high, had only to remind them that "we are not going to make nonconstructive or mean response." Robin and Wilma each assigned a piece of writing very early in the year, returned their students' papers with positive responses, and then asked them how these teacher responses differed from those they had received in the past. Hal provided his students with a handout that explained just how he would respond to their papers. All believed that they needed to begin with teacher response and use it to model the kind of positive response they wanted their students to make to one another's efforts. Teacher response, as used by these four, seemed to include various subcategories such as general affirmative remarks, written responses, and conferences.

General affirmative remarks. The general affirmative remarks began early and seemed to be in an effort to establish a tone of affirmation in their classrooms, or as Wilma put it, at "establishing a safe zone." Wilma would occasionally make remarks such as, "I'm impressed by the level of writing I've been getting. People are letting their voices come through." Robin used such comments more often than the other three. She often said, as she shuffled through a stack of papers, "It looks like there's some neat pieces here," or "I can't wait to get into your files and read your papers. Gosh you guys wrote some neat things. . . . You guys are really doing wonderful with your writing. I hope you realize that." Remarks such as Robin's were intended to suggest that she took the students seriously as writers, affirmed their efforts at writing, and demonstrated an enthusiasm for writing.

Written responses. Most of the response given by these teachers to their students' writing took the form of written marginal or end notes on the students' papers. All used green ink for such comments. "I could use red ink," Robin told her students on the day when she returned their first papers with her comments,

> but since the writing project, red says "negative" to me. I associate red ink with blood. It was discouraging. I went through school not particularly liking to write, because, in part, of that, I think. I know some of you don't particularly care to write. After many years of that, that's not surprising.

These four teachers all reported that their writing project instructors had used green ink to make marginal and end note comments on their papers and that they themselves had not done this until after that experience. "To me green ink says 'positive'," Robin told her students.

Another practice that attempted to "say positive" and was borrowed from their writing project instructors involved the use of underlining and plus signs. As Hal explained, "Whenever I put an underline or a plus sign, it means it's something I like." All of the teachers did this as they read their students' papers.

In general, the teachers' written responses seemed to be one turn in a dialogue that they saw themselves carrying on with their students. As Robin said to her students, "In my response I try to carry on a conversation with you." The teachers' turns in those conversations involved affirmation, personal reaction, questions, and suggestions all in response to either the content or the form of the students' papers.

By way of affirming their students' efforts, they wrote comments such as "Great paper, Susan," "Keep on writing," "Very descriptive," "This is an excellent beginning to your story, Craig," and "This is a very strong piece, Jeremy." Such comments often included the name of the student, just as a speaker might include the name of her listener, and generally appeared as a specific reference along the margins of the paper or as a general comment at the beginning of an end note.

Personal reactions to student papers were often, as Hal told his students, a record of "how your writing affects me, what I think you're trying to say, how your writing makes me feel." Examples of reactive comments included "Yes, it is hard to decide," "I keep trying to figure out what exactly Ralph is . . .," "You have me hauntingly interested," "I was a little confused in the beginning of the story," and "This paragraph builds suspense and makes me want to read more." Again, these often appeared alongside the part of the writing to which they referred or in the end note.

As the year progressed, the teachers began to ask more questions and to make suggestions in their responses to student writing. Such questions might ask, "Is this to confuse any enemies?" "Do you have a plan for such a story?" or "Don't you think your changes make the piece stronger?" Hal shied away from making suggestions, but the others, particularly Eileen, wrote suggestive comments such as, "You might add a little explanation at the beginning about why you are here," or "Explain." Frequently suggestions were offered as questions such as, "Can you tell me more about how you'd do this?" Generally, questions and suggestions seemed directed toward getting the student writers to clarify or expand on something they had said.

Conferences. The third form of teacher response used by Robin, Wilma, Eileen and Hal—the writing conference—was like their general affirmative remarks, oral, but it was also like their written comments, directed at individual students and occurred in one-on-one settings. All four usually held these conferences informally, walking around the room as their students worked, stopping to talk with them for only a minute or two, or conferences were held at their own desks as students sat or stood nearby. Typically, these took place at the teachers' initiation, sometimes at the students'. The teachers' discourse turns in these conferences generally involved affirmation, personal reaction, questions, and suggestions similar to their written comments, but the balance and focus were different. Teacher-initiated conferences at students' desks often involved only brief affirmation and an expression of the teachers' willingness to help, as in "Oh, this looks interesting. How's it going?" Conferences at the teachers' desks—both teacher- and student-initiated—were more likely to focus on a particular part of the paper, to involve perhaps a particular problem, and to involve more questions and suggestions from the teachers. In one conference Eileen told Tammy, "I didn't understand what you said at the beginning. I wondered if you could tell how these two met since that's what your whole story's about."

Although talk about student writing processes fell low on the list of practices that the questionnaire respondents reported using, it seemed to make up a significant part of what happened in these writing conferences. The teachers often asked individual students questions such as, "Why did you write that piece?," "How do you think your writing is going?," "What other pieces have you been working on?," "Where do you get your topics?," and "When do you like to write?" Although all of the teachers asked questions such as these that moved their students to talk about their writing processes, none claimed to be doing it deliberately. "I wasn't aware that I was doing that," Hal said.

In addition to these brief, informal conferences, Hal held longer, more formal ones near the end of the first quarter when he attempted to "get them to say what they think about their writing, what they like, what concerns them. I try hard not to inject my own concerns. . . . I'm trying to get them to see they can re-write." After students had organized their writing folders, they brought them up to Hal's desk for a two- to five-minute conference. Questions comprised most of what Hal said. Student responses were generally brief, one or two words. In one such conference with Julie, Hal's turns consisted of the following:

> You can spell *miscellaneous.* I can't.
> Do you write like this often?
> Why do you do that?
> You said something in that one thing you wrote that you like to write funny. Why do you like to write funny?
> How does this compare with what you wrote last year?
> You weren't happy with it? I remember it was funny.
> How did you come up with those topics?
> Why do you want to write on things nobody else writes on?
> Why?
> Don't do anything to try to please me. Please yourself. That's the person you have to please.

So how do you think your writing is going overall?
Are you happy with it?
So is that part of it not going as well as last year?
Well, thanks for your time. Talk to you next quarter.

These conferences always ended with Hal handing the writing folder back to the student, who had been sitting next to Hal at his desk.

Students seemed to like the positive and the specific nature of their teachers' responses. Tammy, one of Eileen's students, said, "She doesn't just say, 'I like the piece.' She explains why she likes the piece." And Craig, a student of Hal's, said that when he and his classmates get a paper back from Hal,

> he's told us what was good about it, what he really enjoyed about it, what he liked. . . . It [helps because it] points out what my strong points are in writing. And it makes me feel better to know that I can write and someone appreciates my writing. . . . It helps me write more and it makes me feel better. Other teachers told me what was bad about it, what wasn't good about it. That made me want to stop writing.

Like Craig, many of the students reported that previous teachers had focused on their errors. "I like it a lot better in this class," Steven said. They reported that they felt better about themselves as writers—more confident—and that they wrote more, both as a result of the positive response they had received from their teachers. They also felt that their teachers' suggestions and questions were helpful when they revised their writing.

By giving various forms of positive response to their students' writing—general affirmative remarks, written responses, and conferences—the teachers intended to get their students to write and to help them build on their strengths. The general affirmative remarks aided in "establishing a safe zone." Students reported that their teachers' responses helped them to write more than they had in the past, to feel better about their writing abilities, and to revise their writing. Such encouragement and affirmation seemed to be successful. These teachers' use of response—positive response—to their students' writing seemed to be consonant with the writing project principles, and their results seemed to represent their intentions.

Summary

How successful were Robin, Wilma, Eileen, and Hal at implementing their beliefs and intentions? These four—like the other interviewees and the questionnaire respondents—subscribed to the seven writing project principles. As noted earlier, they believed that writing is a complicated process with characteristic stages such as composing, drafting, revising, and editing, and that time must be allowed for these stages. They believed that writers need to write about what's important to them, maintain control over their own processes and products, and that writers need readers to respond to their work—in a positive fashion. They believed that successful writing results more often from attention to meaning than to standard conventions of grammar, spelling, and punctuation. They believed that students learn to write by writing, that students and teachers need to write regularly. Given these beliefs, Robin, Wilma, Eileen, and Hal attempted to create an atmosphere that "make[s] the student want to write." They affirmed their students' efforts by using positive teacher response, then expanded their audience by providing for peer response. Their goal in all this, they reported, was to help their students become "writers and readers."

The teachers' use of journals, support-building practices, and positive response to student writing and the results attained seemed to be consonant with the teachers' beliefs and representative of their intentions. The journals provided for regularity of writing for both students and teachers and generally allowed for student ownership over topics, permitting the students to draw on their own experiences and to write with attention to meaning rather than conventions. When prompts were given, the journals provided another context and purpose for writing, and sometimes journals provided a place for students to reflect on their writing and writing processes.

Another stimulus for such reflection was the writing conference, one of four forms of positive response that the teachers gave to their students' written work. Believing that writers need readers to respond to their work—and that they need these readers to do this positively—the teachers became such readers. Their consistent use of green ink, underlining, plus signs, and marginal and end notes to respond to student writing reminded me of my own post-project practices, indeed of my present response strategies. And their efforts at building support for their teaching resonated with Jerie's "shameless self-promotion" of our Tipton High writing program.

Robin, Wilma, Eileen, and Hal became readers for their students, responding positively and specifically to their efforts, creating atmospheres that encouraged and affirmed those efforts. In these and undoubtedly in other ways, their attempts at moving from belief and intention to practice seemed quite successful.

Chapter Six

Four Teachers Teaching: Problems

Over the course of my visits it also became clear to me that not all of these teachers' practices were as successful as those described in Chapter Five. In two areas the teachers' practices and the results of those practices did not seem to represent their intentions. One involved the use of peer response. The other was less specific; I began to identify it as a kind of general instructional disharmony. This chapter will address these more problematic practices.

Peer Response

In consonance with the fifth writing project principle ("Writers of all ages need readers to respond to their work . . ."), the four teachers were not the only responders in their classrooms; they also made use of peer response to student writing. Results here were mixed.

In all four classrooms the introductions to peer response began as introductions to positive response as given by the teachers. These introductions also began with subtle invitations to the students to read and respond to the work of their classmates. All four teachers posted student writing. Robin had her "Writers' Corner," Wilma displayed "Student Writing," Eileen posted examples of "Eight Kinds of Paragraphs" that had been written by her students, and Hal displayed "Student Writing" in the trophy case outside his room and on his bulletin board. Hal brought this writing to his students' attention:

> Student writing is posted on the bulletin board in the back of the room. It's posted anonymously because I don't want anyone put on the spot or anything. It's also posted in the hall in the trophy case. If you're reading it, don't say anything nasty. The author may be

nearby. They're selected on the basis of subject matter. I hope to post one from each ninth grader. Read them.

Hal typed all of the writing he posted. The others displayed writing just as it had been submitted to them, seldom anonymously. All were concerned, however, that students might say something "nasty" in response to their peers' posted prose.

The move into more formal peer response was more troublesome. Hal preferred to move more slowly than the others and began by having his students respond to pieces that had been written by outsiders so that no one would be injured by any errant criticism. The first time he attempted this, all went as planned. The second attempt, he said later, almost sent him back to the textbooks he had abandoned. Hal gave his students a semi-autobiographical piece he had written, but he did so without attribution, then told them to

(1) Read the piece silently, aloud, or both; (2) In your journals, write your thoughts and reactions to the selection; (3) Select a recorder and a reporter; (4) The reporter is to see that each person tells his/her response to the piece. The recorder is to write down all of the responses; (5) About 9:55 we'll get back into a large group. Each reporter will tell what comments his/her group made.

Hal had his students number off into groups. Chet, in group 4, spoke out as soon as his classmates were seated.

"I'm first. It sucks."

"You have to write in your journal first," Susan stated.

"It's unbelievable," Chet insisted.

"It's boring," Jack said.

"It's got to be nice," Susan said. " You've got to say nice things."

"Do we have to say nice things?" several asked Hal.

"Preferably," Hal said.

Meanwhile, in group 3, the recorder, Angie, began punching Don who punched back. Angie finally stopped long enough to ask each group member, "What do you want put on this paper?" Don asked, "It don't have to be real long, does it?" Later Don quipped, "The only thing salvageable on this piece is the paper." This group made no references to the text.

Group 4, however, did make several references to the words before them.

"Who cares if they're going to the ballgame? It doesn't matter to us," Julie insisted.

"Whoever wrote this," Chet stated, "has a severe mental deficiency."

"It could be somebody in here," Kate suggested.

"Naw," Chet said.

The large group discussion was equally negative, despite Hal's efforts to steer them in another direction through questions, such as, "Suppose you had written this piece and you heard these kinds of comments. How would you feel?" After the students left, Hal fell back in his chair, exhausted. "I've got a lot of work to do with this group," he said.

> I didn't tell them who wrote this piece because I didn't want them to feel bad. I think some of them would have been crushed. I don't want them to start saying good things about writing because any time I pass out anything they suspect I wrote it. . . . Chet was a negative leader in group 4. Julie wouldn't have been so negative if Chet hadn't set the tone. The negative people were so much more vocal. I guess it just reinforces that I need to wait to do peer response. Today would have devastated a kid. Somehow I've got to get them to see that they've got to look for the good and not the bad in what they read. I've got to reshape that negative attitude. It's so typical in schools. Schools are so darned negative. Well, I've got a lot of work to do. No doubt about that. . . . I don't think that piece will die. The kids'll continue to talk about it.

Hal was right; the piece did not die. Even before the day was out, students began to suspect that Hal had written that piece. When his daughter, a student at the school, confirmed that the details of the story matched her family's history, many of the students felt guilty. Several apologized, Julie among them. Later she spoke with me about that class session:

> That time I sort of tore apart his story, I felt really bad about it after I found who it was. And I shouldn't have tore it apart to begin with, but I really felt those things about it. And so the next day I apologized in a way in the writing basket . . . . I don't know what he expected actually. I was being honest.

Hal's problem with errant negativity was not unusual. All of the teachers encountered situations where, despite their efforts at establishing an ethic of affirmation, students did occasionally say negative things about their peers' writing. One day one of Eileen's students passed a response note to one of his classmates that said: "Bill, I didn't like your story. Steve." Eileen was horrified. This was just the sort of "nasty" comment all of these teachers feared, believing that such a response could silence or "devastate" a student writer.

As the teachers saw it, the problem was how "to get them to see that they've got to look for the good and not the bad in what they read . . . [how] to reshape that negative attitude." The teachers wanted honest responses, but they also wanted them to be positive.

In part, the teachers felt students are simply being fourteen-year-olds when they insisted that something "sucks" or "is boring." They also blamed such negativity on the schools, believing, as did the other questionnaire respondents, that schools are "negative places." Julie, too, placed part of the blame there.

> I started out in just a critiquing thing. And maybe it did get a little out of hand. But still those first comments I really thought. . . . I don't know if it would have made any difference, but we did get separated into groups. And that day I was in a certain group with a certain person who is a negative person, and so I think, well, he did it, so we'll just go along. Other people influence you. It's not just you all the time.

Some of these problems with peer response were caused by students' distrust of positive response. After his paper had been read and responded to in a class session, one of Wilma's students, Carl, asked his classmates in exasperation, "Yeah, but is there anything wrong with it? You only tell good things because she says that." Again, Julie spoke to this distrust:

> We're being taught to make sure that there's always something good about it, but in my opinion you always need something bad about it or else there's no room for improvement. . . . We were told to put good comments on it. Even if you hate it to death, you're supposed to find something good in it. And that isn't a bad idea, and I think everybody wants to hear something good about it. But I'd just like, just for once, somebody to tear a piece of my writing apart. Just once. Because you never know if people are telling the truth.

Julie, Carl, and many of the other students found it difficult to trust the response they received because it was always positive. It seemed artificial and imbalanced. They claimed to want to hear something negative.

Another concern expressed by Julie and other students also involved the positive nature of the responses they received: "No one has ever contradicted what I've written. I mean if I got a comment like that or something, then maybe I'd start doing something different." Their teachers expected and encouraged them to revise, but many students felt that the responses they were receiving did not suggest revision. "They just tell you everything's great," one student complained.

Most of the students' responses to their peers' works consisted of general praise and personal reaction, often storytelling ("Yeah, I remember when that happened to me . . ."). When turned loose to respond outside structured settings, it was often difficult to know what had been accomplished. Given a class period for finding peer response, Robin's students one day quickly formed pairs and trios. Chris handed his paper to Jeremy and Chad and said, "I need something to take up space. I wrote it in math class. I had a paper written, but I left it at home." Jeremy and Chad, seeing that the title referred to trout fishing, spent the next fifteen minutes talking about fish, and then helped Chris count his words. They never read his paper. Meanwhile Diane returned Rachel's paper and said, "I like that. You forgot to cross your *t*." Robin, busy helping individuals at her desk, noticed only the quiet interaction and was pleased. "These kids seemed to grasp what it is I wanted them to do," she said. "This is the kind of thing I want going on all the time third quarter."

The intention here is not to denigrate Robin or her students, but to describe what often happened in these classrooms when students were given time for peer response and the teachers were busy conferring with individuals. As the questionnaire respondents and interviewees pointed out, monitoring student activities in a workshop setting can be difficult. Robin had to depend on quick glances to judge the success of the activity. Susan, a student of Robin's, said that most of her responders "just read it and say, 'Oh, that sounds fine.'"

Students, then, developed the idea that if you wanted "real" response, you sought out the teacher. "They don't know what they're talking about," Tammy said of her peers.

> Why should I go to them? I don't think they put their time into writing. When somebody will ask them to read their story, they'll say, "Oh, this is dumb," or something. They won't even care. Mrs. Bauman, she'll look it over and she'll put her ideas and feelings into what she thinks of the story. The kids won't.

Tammy confessed that she continued to ask for response from her classmates because she was supposed to do this, but "then I hand the paper to Mrs. Bauman and let her look it over . . . [before] I write it again."

The teachers' intentions with peer response, then, were to continue "establishing [and maintaining] a safe zone" while providing their writers with more readers who could help them build on their strengths. The results were not always as desired, although sometimes they appeared to be. The teacher response, as described earlier in this chapter, and the posting of student writing seemed to work well. Later, however, the teachers had to deal with "nasty" responses that may have been just as much a product of schooling as of the students' attitudes and ages. The problem became, in part, one of asking the readers to respond honestly yet positively.

The teachers' intentions were thwarted not only by negativity, but also by shallowness. Students complained that their peers gave them flippant or empty responses to their writing, responses that didn't tell them anything, and thus they went to their teachers for "real" response. The teachers, then, busy with individuals, could not monitor the rest of the class.

Some of these problems might have resulted from the speed with which these teachers introduced peer response. Most had their students responding to each other's papers by the second week of classes. Students seemed uncertain about their role as responders. The teachers seemed eager to introduce peer response, perhaps because it had been such an important part of their writing project institute. "I want them to experience what I experienced," Robin said. But as Hal noted, "You can't expect these kids to respond after four weeks the way adult teachers do after three. . . . Maybe it'll take all year. Maybe I should go slow."

General Instructional Disharmony

The second of the two problematic areas involved a collection of instructional practices that seemed dissonant, given the four teachers' stated beliefs and many of their other practices. Among that collection of practices were grading; direct, isolated instruction in grammar, usage, and punctuation; and curricular units of instruction.

Grades were the final form of teacher response to student writing used by these four, although none of them ever spoke of grades as a kind of response. Hal was the only one of the four who never placed a grade on a student paper. Grades for writing in his class were determined solely by the number of papers the student had submitted to the writing basket in a nine-week quarter. Robin asked her students to submit one paper for a quarter grade. Eileen and Wilma each required that one paper be submitted for a grade at the end of their writing units.

In all cases Robin, Eileen, and Wilma had seen and responded to earlier drafts of the papers, which had been submitted for their evaluation. Robin responded in green ink to the papers she graded just as thoroughly as she did with their nongraded papers, then she added a percentage grade, a comment on the quality of editing she had observed in the paper ("good job on editing"), and a circled letter grade in red ink. Eileen, too, wrote percentages atop the papers she evaluated, then she placed an equivalent letter grade alongside. She also wrote brief responses at the ends of these evaluated papers. Wilma wrote brief marginal and end note responses on the papers she graded, then gave twenty points each for "content," "clarity," and "mechanics," and ten points for "focus." She then converted these points into percentages, but not letter grades.

Although the women did not want to grade their students' writing, they felt that it was necessary to do so. "They're such different personalities, such different writers," Robin complained. "You can't assign points to writing," Wilma said. Given this felt responsibility to grade their writing along with the perception that it was a difficult if not impossible task, the teachers fell back on error counting in order to assign points and a grade. Robin explained:

> They know that when I say it's gonna be a graded paper that it's not so much on the content . . . but on the correctness of their writing. It should be a paper that they've worked through. Certainly not a paper in progress, but a paper that they've worked with and taken through enough writing and reworking and paid enough attention to the correctness that it would come up to standard written English level. . . . That lets me off the hook. I still go through those papers even though I've probably read portions of them before, but I still go through and give positive response. But at that point I do also indicate to them spelling errors and anything that would not meet standard English. So I usually figure out some kind of point value per error. . . . I turn them somehow into points, put them on a scale, and give them a grade.

To let themselves "off the hook," the teachers fell back on things like "standard written English" as criterion for evaluation. Becoming an evaluator also changed their role as a responder in that their response needed to justify the grade assigned. Scott, one of Robin's students, explained some of response he received to his quarter paper:

> Here she put down, "I like your description." Right here I shouldn't have put this sentence in. Repeats what I said before. And here she liked these short sentences. Right here she's talking about how I should have used a different word. I didn't explain it good enough. Over here she's correcting a few more mistakes.

Robin, who believed in the power of positive response to "affirm and encourage" and who wanted her students to maintain control of "their own processes and products," found herself in grading papers "correcting . . . mistakes" and telling students that they "shouldn't have put this sentence in" or they "should have used a different word." At the completion of a grading period or unit, roles and rules suddenly changed.

Actually the change may not have been so sudden. Although the teachers said, "You can talk about subjects and verbs but it'll never carry over into their writing," they still made periodic use of large-group, direct instruction in grammar, usage, or punctuation in lieu of the "mini-lessons" and "work with individuals and groups that need a skill" which they had planned. Robin gave her students "writing clean-up sheets." Wilma handed hers a "checklist for proof-reading" one day and spent part of that class period on "there/their/they're," "to/too/two," and "your/you're" before announcing, "I don't think anyone has any problems here."

"As an English teacher, I feel accountable for the correctness of their written expression," Robin explained.

> I have no specific evidence that this is a definite problem. It follows me because I am an English teacher. I like to see things right when I read them. It's a guilt trip that I put on myself. The only person who really heightens this concern of mine is the English teacher these kids go to next. He's a grammarian and very concerned about their correctness. He'll say, "Gosh, how could you stand those freshmen last year the way they do such and such?"

Robin and the others were haunted not always by any real problems in their students' writing, but instead by a feeling of responsibility to their profession, students, and colleagues. English teachers, they felt, are supposed to worry about things like "correctness" and "standard written English."

Another kind of instructional disharmony was reported by the questionnaire respondents who explained that expectations from administrators, parents, and other teachers often pushed them into practices that they no longer valued. Generally Robin, Wilma, Eileen, and Hal were confronted with choices and were aware of the dissonance that resulted in their electing to do other than that in which they believed. But this was not always the case. Robin was one example; her beliefs about writing and the teaching of writing were consonant with those seven writing project principles, and, for the most part, her classroom practices reflected those beliefs.

Three years earlier the school reading committee—on which Robin served, along with her principal, the superintendent, and several other teachers—had turned its attention to what they saw as the "horrendous study habits" of the older students. The committee decided that a study skills unit needed to be incorporated into the ninth-grade English course. Robin, as the freshman instructor, instituted this unit as a semester-long component of her two-semester course. Wanting to get it out of the way so that she could move into a more language-based class, Robin front-loaded the unit, but she kept each Friday aside for writing, seeing that as too important to delay until second semester. On each Friday Robin did what she really loved: taught writing. Her students freewrote, prewrote, rewrote, and responded—and Robin carefully affirmed their efforts.

Robin seemed to have made—in her own mind—a clear distinction between what happened in study skills and what happened in writing workshop. Her students didn't seem to be making that same distinction. Susan, whom Robin described as intelligent and articulate, said that she believed that Robin thought the most important thing for Susan to learn about writing—this after four months of class—was to "be clear and get down to the main idea" and "taking notes and being organized." "She's always talking about study skills and how we should be organized," Susan explained.

Eileen and Wilma also operated within traditional notions of curriculum, teaching individual instructional units. Although they valued writing and enjoyed teaching it, writing still remained only one or two of several units. Wilma told her students as they grew impatient with their library skills unit, "I don't want to spend a lot of time on it. We have a lot more important things to do than be saddled with a library unit." Later, after class, she announced, "I hate this library skills unit." Yet she began the school year with it. After ending her second unit, the one on writing, Wilma said:

> Some kids didn't write and feel good about their writing. That bothers me. . . . If they have more opportunities to write, kids'll eventually come up with something they're proud of, but I can't afford the time because I feel that in ninth grade I need to expose them to various genres of literature and other stuff.

As important as she believed writing and allowing time for writing is, Wilma left it behind because she also felt a responsibility to "expose" her students to poetry, novels, and short stories. Less enthusiastic about these units, she moved through them more quickly, often barely integrating writing. As a result, writing still remained slotted into specific instructional units.

So a second problem area was the general instructional disharmony that resulted from the teachers' practices regarding grading; punctuation, grammar, and correctness; and the use of instructional units. The teachers were haunted by notions of accountability and responsibility. They wanted their students to control "their own processes and products"; they believed that writing and allowing time for writing were important; they believed that good writing results more often from attention to meaning than from standard conventions of language. At the same time, they also believed that they had to give and justify a grade for writing; they felt responsible for "expos[ing]" their students "to various genres and other stuff"; they felt "accountable for the correctness of their [students'] written expression." Because of these and undoubtedly other factors, then, some of their efforts at implementation were not completely successful.

Summary

Peer response was clearly more problematic than teacher response. The teachers' intentions here were to provide their writers with more readers who could help them build on their strengths, while at the same time continuing to establish and maintain an encouraging and affirming environment. The results were mixed, as Jake and Sally, two of my interviewees, suggested in Chapter Three. Teacher response and the posting of student writing seemed to work well. Later, however, the teachers and students had to deal with negative, shallow, and flippant responses that may have been a product of schooling; the students' attitudes, ages, and uncertainty about their role as responders; and the speed with which the teachers introduced peer response. In part, the difficulty became one of asking the readers to respond honestly yet positively. Many students went to their teachers for "real" response, who then were too busy to monitor the rest of the class. The teachers seemed eager to introduce peer response, perhaps because it had been such an important part of their writing project institutes.

Another problem area came from the teachers' practices regarding grading, language conventions, and the use of instructional units. The teachers were haunted by contradictory beliefs and notions of accountability and responsibility; this resulted in a kind of general instructional disharmony: they wanted their students to control their own writing; they believed that writing is valuable and that attention to meaning rather than to standard conventions of language is more important, yet they also believed that they had to give and justify a grade for writing, they felt responsible for spending class time on the various genres of literature, and they felt "accountable for the correctness" of their students' writing. Some of the teachers' efforts at implementation were therefore problematic.

Again, these teachers' experiences helped me appreciate the "domed environment" that I had enjoyed in my post-project teaching at Tipton. Our English curriculum had me teaching courses given completely to writing, allowing me to avoid isolating writing within individual curricular units. We could take our time with writing because we had an entire semester given over to it. There was no pressure to move on into literature or library skills units.

Neither was there much pressure to teach traditional school grammar or be "accountable for the correctness" of my students' written expression. Jerie Weasmer, my colleague and department chair, had thrown out the grammar books. Grades in our courses were determined in large measure by student self-assessment using willingness to revise one's own writing and respond to others' writings as criteria.

Peer response, however, was sometimes troublesome. My students, like those of these four teachers, seemed inclined toward negative criticism ("That sucks."), general praise, and vague comments ("I like it. It's nice."). I can still hear myself repeatedly insisting that "Good response is positive and specific." We spent a great part of the year using the whole class as our only peer response setting because I often didn't feel I could trust my students to operate in small groups or pairs without me. And my students, too, often distrusted the positive response they received from their peers and from me. "Tell me what you *really* think," they'd insist, a plea that I grew to hear instead as "Persuade me that you really do like my writing."

Chapter Seven

Four Teachers Tell Their Stories

Almost three years after my semester of observation in their class-rooms, I invited Hal, Wilma, Eileen, and Robin to reconsider their professional lives before and after the writing project, to think about what it meant to them to have been a case study subject, and to tell the stories of their classroom lives since then. This chapter, then, is authored by these four teachers. Hal's story runs throughout and is punctuated by excerpts from the stories composed by Robin, Eileen, and Wilma.

Background

My name is Hal Thompson; I began teaching at twenty-one immedi-ately after graduating from college in 1969. In those days, undergrad-uate teaching candidates were not encouraged to have minors; in fact, we were encouraged to concentrate on our major field only. As a result, I finished school certified to teach nothing but French at the secondary level, and that is what I did for the next thirteen years at Stone Creek Junior and Senior High Schools. I taught through the era of enrollment decline and budget cuts, frequently fearing for my job since foreign languages were often on the chopping block in those days, and I could teach nothing else. Finally all the years of fighting for my job and raising funds to take my French classes on trips to Quebec in order to keep my class sizes up took its toll.

When a junior high language arts teacher resigned in 1982, I quickly discussed with my junior high principal the possibility of my transferring to that job. While I could legally teach nearly any subject, including language arts, at either the seventh- or eighth-grade level, my lack of proper certification was a problem for the school's accreditation status. After considerable discussion with the school administration and acceptance to a graduate program in English at the nearby University of Iowa, I was given a position as half-time language arts, half-time French teacher at the junior high with the understanding that I earn an English endorsement as soon as possible. The following year saw me begin a "new" teaching career and resume my education in a brand new field.

While I began teaching English with virtually no college English courses to my credit, I really felt no great fear. After all, I had taught a language for thirteen years, and in that time I had formulated several ideas about how English should be taught. I had not been shy about stating that junior high and high school students ought to be taught more grammar. For many years I had found myself teaching English grammar in order to teach French. I *knew* what English teachers should be doing, and now I had the chance to correct the past errors of my colleagues. As an English teacher, I intended to teach grammar and mechanics and lists of spelling words. And I did just that. My students used *Warriner's* and diagrammed sentences and did drill after drill on parts of speech and sentence patterns. We studied topic sentences, detail sentences, clincher sentences, and five-paragraph themes. We drilled on long lists of spelling words and took a spelling test each Friday. I taught English the way it "ought" to be taught.

The one thing my students didn't do a lot of was write. I found it terribly boring to read all those papers on the same topic, and it took forever to correct all those mistakes with my red pen. It was sheer drudgery to point out mistakes and make my students correct them before turning in a final draft of their papers nicely written in ink. Since assigning writing and then grading it was such a pain, I assigned very little. And as that first year progressed, fewer and fewer of the papers that were assigned ever found their way back to the students. In fact, more than one set of papers mysteriously got lost. But so what, I thought. I was teaching English, the important things at least, the way I felt it should be taught, and I felt neither guilt nor inadequacy.

My first few graduate English courses did nothing to change my mind. I was studying Shakespeare, British and American literature, adolescent literature, and I even had to take a graduate level grammar course, which I of course found very easy, especially after years of drilling teenagers on those very points. My grammar professor did ask the class members how often we had our students write, but since I considered grammar drills writing, I missed the point of her question and responded that my students wrote frequently. It wasn't until I enrolled in a master's degree seminar that the message began to make its way into my thick skull.

Our instructor for that course had us read and study a great deal of the literature available concerning the teaching of English and the teaching of writing. Almost every piece of research I read indicated that teaching grammar was not teaching writing and had very little effect, if any, on a student's ability to write. Even studies done at the turn of the century had demonstrated that fact, but still teachers felt that grammar instruction was crucial in the teaching of English, even though it was painfully obvious that American students were poor writers and showing little progress. The message had at last entered my consciousness, and the more courses I took in search of my endorsement and degree, the more I began to believe it.

The problem I faced was that no course gave me any ideas or suggestions about what to teach or how to teach English so that the students' writing skills would show improvement. I simply did not know what to do differently than what I had been doing. The other language arts teachers I knew were doing nearly the same things that I was doing. In fact, we were in the process of rewriting our district language arts curriculum, and the new curriculum turned out to be heavily weighted toward skills—grammar, mechanics, spelling. Few of us in the district knew how to break the habits that had gripped the English curriculum in our schools for a century or more. Then the writing project came into my life.

Our school district was sending five teachers each summer to the Iowa Writing Project and paying the tuition for the course as well as all of the expenses for the fall writing project conference. The deal was too good to pass up, especially since the course fit right into my graduate studies.

That three-week class turned out to be the best I had ever had at the graduate level. We learned a host of teaching techniques by actually experiencing those techniques being used on us. We read and studied the ideas of writing experts. We became a family, and we learned that creating a family atmosphere in our classrooms was a major tool in teaching our students to write. We wrote, and through the instructor's responses to our writing, our self-esteem was boosted to the point that even the most reluctant of writers among us began to feel comfortable as writers. We learned the difference between revising and editing, and we learned the place of each of those skills in our classrooms. In time virtually everyone in the class began to realize that the best way to teach English was to teach writing and that grammar drills were not helpful or necessary in the teaching of writing. All of us had improved as writers over that three-week period, not by studying grammar but by writing. At last, someone

I'm not quite sure what I did in the seven years of full-time teaching before my first experience with the writing project. It seems so long ago, and, in a sense, it really was. I do, however, remember it involved a series of grammatical hoop jumping, administrative commandeering, test teaching, textbook square dancing, and silent questioning by me. Only the closest of my colleagues were privy to my whispered tones of dissatisfaction with the way we handled writing, reading, thinking, and learning.

I thought I was doing an adequate job, but I could tell my students weren't keying in. I knew that the barren, endless drilling on grammar exercises, spelling lists, and out-of-context vocabulary words were activities that merely took students through the paces. My hope was that some day a student here and there might remember and apply this work when using language in context. Any way I looked at it, I was dissatisfied with my methods. But, I reasoned that student performance on standardized tests and college entrance exams might reach acceptable levels if I drilled and killed them; so I did. After all, the scores on those tests were how students and teachers were evaluated. Who was I to upset that?

It would seem logical that if I were dissatisfied with pat literature textbook selections, directed questions at the end of each piece, five-paragraph essays, spelling lists, grammar and usage exercises, and vocabulary out of context, that dissatisfaction alone would propel me to change. But change to what? Replace these practices with what? Most of the models paralleled what I was doing. I taught how I was taught, how I was expected to teach. As far as I knew, my regimented way of teaching was the only way. Who was I to question tradition?

I thought that my hunches about some students' turned-off attitudes, lack of serious motivation, and ennui toward formulaic approaches to language arts just suggested that I just wasn't very good at what I did. I attempted to dismiss my unease; mediocre was probably the best I could be. I just wasn't pedagogically fit. And I probably still wouldn't be without the writing project. Actually, I didn't know much about the writing project before I signed up. I was intrigued by the questionnaire that asked about my own history as a teacher and my teaching practices with regards to the teaching of writing. I took the class because I was curious.

—Wilma

was not only teaching us what to teach, but also how to teach it. It was a great summer, and I could hardly wait for school to start so I could use my new found ideas and methods in my own classroom. What a poor, though well-intentioned, teacher I had been. Many of us in that summer course mentioned that we felt we owed our former students an apology for the horrors we had put them through and the disservice we had done them. At least we wouldn't make those same mistakes again in the years to come.

Or so I thought. Even though I entered my classroom the following fall with great enthusiasm and many new ideas, I soon found myself slipping back into my old ways. You see, our writing project lasted three weeks, and I was facing thirty-six weeks of school. Our writing project was full of people who were anxious and willing to try new things and to learn; my classes were full of adolescents. In fewer than nine weeks, I had used up all of the ideas I had been exposed to in my writing project, and I didn't know how to proceed. Oh sure, we were still writing in our journals for five minutes every day, the students were still being allowed to choose their own topics and styles, and I was still using my green pen and positive comments and returning all my students' papers promptly. And my students were actually writing much more than ever before, so I *had* made some progress. But we were still doing those awful grammar drills and spelling lists and vocabulary exercises with more words than any genius could learn at one time. I didn't feel good about doing that, but I had to do something in order to keep the students busy and under control. I still did not know how to organize and manage a language arts classroom without relying on a textbook and a teacher's manual. I knew I was missing the boat, but I could find no way to get aboard the vessel I wanted to ride. So the following summer, I signed up for IWP Level II, at my own expense. Surely I would find the answers to my problems in that course, I thought.

Level II was only a two-week course, but it gave each class member the opportunity to explore whatever area of writing instruction he or she felt was most necessary. I was so confused by my experiences of the previous school year that I wasn't sure what avenue to pursue. It was comforting, however, when we all began to share our frustrations and failures in putting our writing project ideals to work in our classrooms. It was comforting to realize that I wasn't the only person who had been unable to change my ways. I shared what *had* worked for me, and I learned what had worked for others. I also met a person or two who weren't buying into the writing project philosophy completely, and in discussing and debating with these nonbelievers, I was able to put my own beliefs and thoughts into far clearer form for myself. Once again I looked forward to the coming school year and yet another opportunity to improve my teaching style.

The next fall I still wasn't able to shake all my bad habits, however. I had learned how to manage my classroom somewhat better, and I no longer tried to move so quickly. Nine weeks came and went, and I still had some tricks up my sleeve. Unfortunately, I was still

Going into the classroom and attempting to initiate new methods for teaching writing and developing new classroom structures was not as easy as I had hoped it would be. I knew that I wanted my students to make choices about their writing. I wanted them to see themselves as writers and feel they were a part of a positive, supportive community of writers. Unfortunately, I was not always able to create this atmosphere because I did encounter reluctant writers. My students also proved to be ineffective and sometimes even insensitive responders to each other's work.

I struggled with various ways for them to respond. I modeled, gave them response forms to follow, and frequently discussed the need for the students to be supportive and specific with their responses. I also struggled with ways for them to find meaningful writing topics and ways for them to be published in hopes that this would help motivate them to continue writing. Keeping up with the amount of writing being accomplished was another difficult task I faced as I began using writing workshops. Recreating the writing project structure I had experienced was not always possible because of time. I wanted to conference but had difficulty accomplishing this as often as I would have liked. Journals were also difficult to keep up with. I believe journaling is an extremely effective learning tool, but I often felt uncomfortable with the information the students would share openly and often quite graphically with me. On the other hand, I was disappointed with some students who seemed to say very little in their journals and found them to be a total waste of time. It was as though journals were either invaluable or totally useless.

I also struggled with how I could effectively teach mechanics, grammar, usage, vocabulary, and spelling without falling back on drills from worksheets and textbooks. I felt quite successful dealing with some of these skills while conferencing, but I was not able to conference as often as I felt I should.

Another frustrating factor for me was that there was not another faculty member at my school who had experienced the writing project. I would have liked to have had someone to talk with about the problems I was encountering.

The positive things that were happening, however, were greater than the frustrations I encountered. I loved the fact that my students were writing and sharing. They were trying to find their own voices, and they were often successful in very moving and powerful pieces. I loved that my students had pride in their work, that many of their pieces were published, and that I eventually even had one student who hoped to become a professional writer. Writing became a worthwhile product and most of my students, I believe, did view themselves as writers.

—*Eileen*

too dependent on that old, familiar textbook and those drills. I religiously stayed away from the grammar drills and sentence diagramming, but my students still were plagued with the drills on punctuation, capitalization, and other types of mechanics. They still were "learning" long lists of obscure spelling words. I justified that to myself by reasoning that since my students had to take the Iowa Tests of Basic Skills each year, drilling on mechanics and spelling could do no harm and might even help.

I did enroll in IWP Level III during the fall of that year. Level III met one evening every other week, and the emphasis of the course was on keeping a journal of the things we were doing in our classrooms. I found this to be very valuable because it made me consciously think about my procedures and my reasons for doing various things in the classroom. One of the major adjustments I made as a result of my journaling was to organize my classes so that only one group of students turned in papers for me to read on any one day. Before, I had been getting fifty or more papers on some days, and I would stay up till all hours to get them responded to for the next day. Through discussions with myself in my journal and with my colleagues in the Level III class, I developed a better-paced and more manageable system.

Level III also allowed me to share what was working for me and to pick up ideas about what was working for others. I found that many of us were still struggling to put our beliefs into practice. We had made some progress, but most of us were still much more textbook-dependent than we really wanted to be. There was a considerable gap between our beliefs and our practices, but most of us had learned to accept that gap as something with which we could live. I think I felt at that point in my teaching career that I had made about all the progress I could make. I was a better teacher than I had been, but I still wasn't quite where I felt I should be. Unfortunately I was out of

---

Because I had such a great experience in Level I, but knew I still needed to learn so much more about how to deal with the problems I had, I enrolled in Level III a year later. This course was the most worthwhile class I have ever taken because I had an audience for what I was doing in the classroom. Journaling about my classroom helped me solve my problems. It also encouraged me to re-think what I was doing, and when something did go well, it often enabled me to see why it worked.

—Eileen

---

writing project courses now, and the prospects for additional change on my part appeared to be slim. Then Dave Wilson sent me his questionnaire.

My Experience as a Research Subject/Participant

I was flattered and pleased to fill out the questionnaire and be a part of Dave's project. The questions gave me an opportunity to wax eloquent on my newly formed philosophy about the teaching of writing. I didn't know Dave personally at this time, but his name had come up frequently in various writing project discussions, so I knew of him. But not being actually acquainted with Dave gave me the opportunity to be rather idealistic in my answers. As I recall, I didn't really have to delve too deeply into the discrepancy between my beliefs and my practices. That's the beauty of answering questionnaires; you need only write down what you want the reader to know. However, that luxury disappeared when Dave phoned and asked to set up a personal interview.

I remember feeling very nervous and intimidated as Dave sat in my living room one summer afternoon and quizzed me about my ideas, beliefs, and experiences. Perhaps it was the presence of his tape recorder, or perhaps it was just the experience of meeting an IWP "expert" face-to-face. I made it through the interview, though, because Dave's manner put me at ease almost at once. I still felt that I rather understated the fact that my beliefs and my actual practices weren't quite identical, to put it mildly, but then who doesn't try to

---

I remember receiving the survey Dave sent and thinking it could be from someone who was adverse to the writing project and its philosophies. I answered the questions vehemently, ready to wholeheartedly defend the project. Later, of course, I realized this wasn't the case, and when Dave asked me for an interview, I was really excited and interested. I enjoyed talking about what I believed and thinking about the questions he asked.

I remember one question in particular disturbed me. He asked if I encouraged others to participate in the writing project. I told him that I really didn't feel that I openly promoted it. Later, I felt guilty about this. It made me feel as though I was doing the writing project a disservice because I really believed it was a tremendously effective and worthwhile experience. Later on I did encourage colleagues to participate in the project and one eventually did complete Level I.

—Eileen

make reality sound a bit better than it really is? And who would ever know? Little did I know at that time that I would become one of the four teachers Dave would visit the following year.

Not being one to say "no" and being egotistical enough that the prospect of being a part of a doctoral dissertation was quite appealing, I readily agreed to allow him to visit my classes for a semester.

My first period journal entry from the day that Dave made his first visit reads: "I'm anxious about the day, but not really nervous." But by sixth period on the same day, my comments were as follows:

It was shortly before my tenth year of teaching was to begin. I faced one major change in my schedule, a second section of creative writing in addition to my normal duties of the past few years, which included creative writing, three sections of freshmen English, one section of journalism, one section of publications, the newspaper, yearbook, and contest large group speech. Dave Wilson's phone call that August presented another change or addition to the first semester that I had not anticipated. I hesitated to agree to being a research subject. Inside, I wondered how much more work this was going to require of me and what could I possibly have to contribute to research and did I really want someone watching me teach or observing my students' behavior and performance in the classroom. Even after nine years of teaching and the Iowa Writing Project behind me, I still often felt a lack of confidence in myself, in my teaching of writing. Making a difference in the lives of hundreds of teenagers is an incredible responsibility, and although I wanted to give each a valuable writing learning experience in my classroom, there were plenty of days that I questioned if what I were asking them to do was worthwhile. Was there enough writing, too much writing, meaningful writing? Was my response specific enough, too much response, not enough? How about the freedom to choose topics? General guidelines, no guidelines, specific topics for those who struggled? At what point do I work with correcting writing? Editing? Revising? Some students accept that portion of the writing process more easily or sooner than the reluctant writers. I had read, written, and talked about these questions during IWP and since, but every school year new groups of students brought them to the surface again. Dave's presence meant that I might be discovered as an IWP failure. I believed that I was surely doing it wrong or halfway. I didn't admit these reservations to Dave, and since we had taken the writing project together, I said yes, if it would help him out. I remained skeptical, yet a part of me was hopeful—hopeful that Dave would bring ideas, change, something new to this staling teacher in Room 118.

—Robin

When Dave asked to observe my classes, I immediately said yes. I couldn't wait for the opportunity to have someone to talk with about what I was trying to accomplish. I did feel a bit nervous about having someone come into my classroom, but I think I believed this would be a learning experience for me as well. Having Dave observe my classes proved to be one of the most positive experiences I have had in my teaching career. I felt his presence subtly encouraged the students to examine what they were doing in my classroom, and helped me to believe what I was attempting was worthwhile and important. The students also, I believe, enjoyed having someone come into their very small rural classroom. I think they became more interested in what was happening because someone else was interested in their accomplishments.

—Eileen

"I wish I knew what was going on in Dave Wilson's mind. It's a bit unnerving to have him sitting here, writing in his notebook, and never knowing what's going on." I was indeed nervous and more than a bit intimidated by Dave's presence. It was the first week of a new school year, I was dealing with a whole group of new faces, and suddenly the discrepancy between my beliefs and my practices was on the verge of being discovered. Yes, I had reason to be nervous.

My goal for this particular semester was to bring my beliefs and my practices into line. I felt as if I had to do that or be discovered for the fraud I was. My journal entries for the next few days of school, when Dave wasn't present, show that I did begin to try to practice what I believed. I had real incentive to do that because I knew that he would be observing me once a week or more for several months to come. My September 11 journal entry for first period, however, hinted at what was really to take place: "Dave Wilson is here and he says he will pick either first or second period to observe on a permanent basis. I'm glad it won't be my last two classes; they would not work well in the study, I'm afraid. I'm partial to second period myself, but either of the first two would be okay." I was about to change my practices all right, but only for one period a day. My seventh period journal entry reads: "Dave Wilson left towards the end of third period today. He had lots of questions for me and took lots of notes. I really can't read him as far as what he's thinking. I don't know if I come off as a real ninny or in a positive manner. I may never know. He has decided to limit his visits to the second period class, however. So I need to keep that in mind when I plan their lessons next week." The stage was set. The fraud would continue.

I did indeed make a conscious effort to put my beliefs into practice during that second period class, but mainly on the days when I
knew Dave would be present. Witness my second period journal
entry for September 16:

> Dave is here. I hope this experiment of mine goes well. It's some-
> thing I probably wouldn't have normally done today, but yet it's
> something I want to try. I want the emphasis of my class to be on
> writing and reading, so I need to slowly head in that direction. And
> there are lots of other things going on here, too . . . work on listen-
> ing skills, work on speaking skills, work on writing skills, work on
> persuading your audience about your point of view, etc. I hope it
> works. I really would like to read to my classes fairly regularly, but
> I haven't been able to for several years. Now maybe I can.

My experiment that day was to read aloud to my class a story
that had no ending. When I finished reading, I had the students write
a brief ending in their journals, and then we discussed the various
possibilities. I hadn't been able to read aloud for about four years due
to voice problems, but those problems had cleared up over the summer, and I was finally willing to take the chance of doing some oral
reading. The experiment did work out fairly well that period, but
that was the only period during the day that I did that particular
exercise. Dave's presence in my room forced me to put aside the old
English text, the drill work, all the old practices, and to try something much more consistent with my writing project beliefs. But I
still had only enough courage to do that during the one period or
more each week when I was being observed.

And so the semester continued. I experimented with that second
period class, while—unbeknownst to Dave—doing little different in
my other classes. Although I felt more than a bit hypocritical, the
seeds of a more complete change in my teaching style were being
sown. On October 1, I wrote in my journal at the end of second
period: "Dave Wilson is here again. I'm glad he's been coming. His
presence has given me the incentive to spend more time on writing-
types of activities and less on other things. I'd like to do that more
and more in most of my classes." And then later that same day: "I
had a nice visit with Dave Wilson this morning. I still don't know
what he's thinking, but it's nice to be able to bounce ideas off him
anyway. He's an excellent listener."

Even though my practices were bordering on the hypocritical
that semester, I don't think I was trying to fool Dave anymore. I
remember discussing with him the fact that I would love to be able
to teach English without using a text, but that I just didn't know how
to pull it off. Dave didn't attempt to tell me how to accomplish my

From my teaching journal:

9-8 "Dave will be a catalyst for my writing and planning. I always work a little harder if I know someone (a peer) is watching. His presence will force me to be more polished—more prepared—in teaching and in writing. I want to process enough writing to share with my classes for silent readings . . . after all, their response to my writing is part of what draws me closer to them and is part of the excitement I experience in the classroom."

9-25 "So far . . . so good! I liked today's writing lesson. It felt right to me, Lord. Please continue to guide me in what to do with and say to these young writers. They are all so unique . . . all have so much to say . . . may we continue to grow with one another in our writing. Thanks for sending Dave . . . his insight and involvement renew my interest and effort to try new techniques."

10-19 "Freshmen are working on quarter papers . . . goal of a first rough draft by end of today's class period. Further step-by-step preparation needed . . . hopeful this time in preparation gives them successful results on final drafts. . . ."

". . . I didn't do this, not this way, last year. Dave's presence has forced me to be more accountable about the teaching of writing. He asks why I do the things I do."

—Robin

goal, but he did listen to my ideas and reassured me that I wasn't the only person to be going through the inner turmoil I felt. The goal I had in mind for myself was not an easy one to accomplish. I began to feel not so much a "fraud" as a teacher fighting to shake off the chains of a past that had had English teachers in its grip for many years.

The reassurance Dave gave me helped me struggle on through the semester. On October 8, I wrote at the beginning of second period: "Dave Wilson is here. I've come to look forward to this day with this class. I think I'm learning from it, and I hope the kids are picking up some things, too." Being a part of this research project had definitely become a learning experience for me. I was experimenting, trying new things, actually putting my beliefs into practice at least for one period a week. That didn't seem like much at the time, but it was a start. Knowing that I was going to be observed regularly kept me creative and made me think seriously about the teaching of English. While the purpose of Dave's visits was not to create change in my style and performance, they were doing exactly that. I was aware of that, and I was concerned about what would happen once Dave stopped showing up in my room. On December 7, I wrote: "Dave is done with me now. He will finish up the other two schools

---

Dave's desire to do case studies in my room was provocative. I wasn't really nervous about him being there. I welcomed his presence because I knew that our experiences in the project were similar.

During the semester of visits, his presence in the back of the room became less and less noticeable. Subconsciously, though, I think I was very much aware of him. His image was there when I planned the lessons. His presence was there as he sat recording what I said and did. Because of this, I was less apt to lapse into my old ways during his study. He knew of my dissatisfaction with my teaching practices, and, quite frankly, I didn't want to appear hypocritical. I admit that before the study I was coasting a bit. Although I was dissatisfied with some of my methods, I am chagrined to say it was easier to hold fast to old ways. It took courage, energy, and time to develop different and better approaches—three ingredients that I have little of. But I said "yes" to Dave's project and decided to give it a complete go.

Dave's eyes were like another pair of eyes looking at what I was doing. And that was good. His presence enabled me to uncover forming beliefs and deal with nagging issues like teaching usage and grading. His presence helped me review my teaching much like I had reviewed my writing after Cleo wrote her responses. What I thought I did well I wanted to continue, and what I didn't do well—according to my evaluation—I had a strong desire to improve upon. Although Dave was totally nonjudgmental and rather annoyingly close-mouthed, his observing acted as a catalyst enabling me to dispel stale practices and replace them with fresh ideas. His searching provided credence to my forming beliefs about the teaching of writing and literature. After all, if it were worth investigating and researching, it was worth my mulling over.

—Wilma

---

this week and the fourth next week. I hope I get a chance to read his work when it's done. And I really hope I don't get away from what I'm doing, now that he won't be coming."

Effect of the Study on My Process of Change

Dave's study had a great effect on me and on the process of my change as an English teacher. From the very beginning when I filled out the original questionnaire, Dave's questions made me analyze and reanalyze my beliefs about the teaching of English.

Graduate school courses had made me aware of the faulty ideas I had formulated as an observer of English teachers, and the writing project courses had begun to show me how I could be an effective

English teacher. It wasn't until Dave walked into my room, however, that I began to reanalyze my practices, what I was really doing in the classroom. I began to justify every move I made, both to myself and to Dave. Mind you, Dave seldom asked for any justification. He occasionally asked me why I chose to do something, but he never criticized me or made me feel that I was doing something wrong. I began to feel, however, that I owed him an explanation for my every move. I felt guilty if I relapsed into textbook drills or if I did something that I knew was not relevant to the goals I had in mind. I wanted to please Dave and my writing project mentors, and I wanted to be an effective English teacher, an effective writing teacher. Dave Wilson's project was the catalyst I needed to make some concrete changes in my teaching practices. I felt that Dave *was* the Iowa Writing Project come to life for me. He was knowledgeable and supportive and caring. He was the one person I could talk to during the day who understood my problems and who could help me with that self-esteem built way back in Level I. Dave gave me the incentive I needed to put my beliefs to work in my classroom.

I still think about Dave and his project as I plan and carry out my lessons. I try to be ready to explain or justify my every move as I was when I knew Dave would be present. But instead of telling Dave why I'm doing what I'm doing, I now tell my students so that they have some idea of what we're trying to accomplish and how what we're doing should help them grow and learn. I continue to write in my journal with my students each and every class period. I chronicle what I've done in class, how it went, and what things I might try to change for the next class period, the next week, the next year. I strive to grow and to change and to bring my practices and beliefs more closely into line. I've not reached perfection yet; I know that perfection is not attainable. But I have grown and changed a great deal as a language arts teacher in the past few years, and I continue to grow with each passing class period. And I am convinced that my participation in this research project has been a major reason for my ability to continue to change. I had reached a dead end after IWP Level III. Dave Wilson opened a new avenue for me to explore.

And so continued the semester, snatches of ideas and observations in my journal paired with Dave's visits sustained my involvement in what I was doing and why I was doing it. At times I wondered what the semester would have been like without the ongoing research project. I'm certain that it served as a shot in the arm.

—*Robin*

*Overall having Dave visit my classroom was extremely benefi-
cial for me at the time. I had a chance to discuss the problems I was
dealing with, and his presence in the classroom helped to justify
what I was trying to accomplish. Although my colleagues did not
teach as I did, Dave's visits reinforced my credibility as a teacher
and the methods I used. The visits also encouraged me to continue to
look at what I was doing and how someone else might view my practices. Therefore, I was constantly seeking answers to my problems
and mentally explaining what I was attempting to do. Justifying my
methods became very important to me, and this remains true to this
day.*

—*Eileen*

Changes I've Experienced Since
the Semester of Dave's Visits

As I mentioned when discussing Dave's original questionnaire, it's
pretty easy to be selective when putting things on paper with the
thought that no one will ever be around to check them out. I think
I've outgrown that, however, partially as a result of my experience
with Dave and his project. I have more confidence in myself these
days. I'm not afraid to experiment with something new, and I'm not
afraid to fail. I recently began teaching an IWP Level III seminar of
mv own. Being in charge of that class has led me back to my own
Level III journals and has helped me to continue to experiment and
grow. I have some ideas and suggestions for the teachers in my class,
but I also learn a lot from them. I've come to the conclusion that the
day I feel I have all the answers is the day I'll walk out the door, no
longer able to be an effective teacher.

I no longer use a language text or a spelling text in my ninth-
grade language arts classes. I succeeded in eliminating the use of a
text in my classroom beginning with the school year following
Dave's visits. In fact, during the second semester of the year in which
Dave was in my room, I began to wean myself from the text, and I
made a complete break the following fall. I do make use of a program
called *Daily Oral Language* (DOL), however. In this program, two
sentences that contain some grammatical and usage errors and that
are completely devoid of capital letters or punctuation are given to
the students each day. Their task is to write the sentences correctly;
when the students finish, we quickly go over the sentences and discuss the changes that needed to be made. I use this program for a
couple of reasons. One is that I still feel some pressure from parents
and the school administration to teach mechanics and grammar. The

The year following Dave's study I enrolled in Level III of the writing project. It allowed me to journal and reflect on my teaching practices daily. My curiosity was heightened, my appetite sufficiently whetted. Dave's presence helped me become actively interested in seeking out what I could do better in the classroom. The course, which met over an entire year of school, provided me with the opportunity to look at and record what I was doing. This allowed deeper reflecting on my classroom practices. Response to these journal entries helped form answers to some of those very first nagging questions. The Level III course was perhaps the most solid impetus to change in my practices. What that class did was help me see more clearly. It helped me throw out what I didn't feel comfortable with and replace those stale practices with more solid ways. It made me become a more focused teacher, and helped me align my teaching practices with what I truly believed they should be.

—Wilma

Daily Oral Language system allows me to do this while using only five to ten minutes of class time each day. The second reason is that this program gives me what I feel is an excellent method of beginning class each day. I have the sentences on a transparency showing on the screen as the students enter the room. The students know that they are to get right to this task, and most do so immediately. I use this time to take attendance, discuss make-up work with those who have been absent, and take care of those mundane tasks that rob all of us of valuable class time. I feel that the time we use for these sentences and the resultant review of grammar and mechanics would normally be wasted anyway. *DOL* has given me a way to make productive use of the opening minutes of class and at the same time to satisfy the desires of those who feel that grammar and mechanics should be taught. I must point out, however, that I have seen absolutely no benefit to my students' writing from this exercise. We can discuss subject-verb agreement during *DOL* time, for example, and in the writing done later on the same period, a number of students will make the very mistake we've just talked about. There is not and never will be a correlation between teaching grammar and mechanics and teaching students to write, no matter the methods used. I am solidly convinced of that.

The thing that does help students learn to write is for them to write often. Therefore, we write in our journals nearly every day of the year. The last five minutes of class is set aside for both my students and me to simply write about whatever is on our minds. My classes and I have been doing this since I finished my original writing project.

We also use our journals to record thoughts and impressions about the stories and books we read in class; this use of our journals has increased a great deal since my participation in Dave's project. When I decided to eliminate the language text from my classroom, I had to find something to fill the void. Being unable and unwilling to read the papers generated by having students write every day (I'm no martyr, you see), I began to have my students read more good literature than I had ever considered having them read previously. We had no time to read great books and stories when we had all those grammar drills and spelling words to do, so we read very little. (Talk about needing to apologize to former students! How I missed that boat for so long, I'll never know.) Now, however, our entire secondary language arts staff has met and mapped out the books and stories to be read at each level so that we avoid overlap and still cover those works to which we feel all students should be exposed. And instead of page after page of questions to answer about each chapter or group of pages in the things I assign to be read, we use our journals to record our thoughts and ideas. As a result, my students write more, and I hope think more about what they're reading. I attempt to look through each student's journal once a month. I ask the students to mark an entry or two for me to read and comment on, but otherwise I just glance through the journal to be sure that everyone is indeed writing as instructed.

Another change I have made in my classes since Dave was present is an increase in the use of peer response. I have used peer response since my first experience with the writing project, but it was one of those things that seemed to run its course in about nine weeks. Since the semester of Dave's visits, I have begun to use peer response in a wider variety of ways, and more importantly, I think, I have begun to explain to the students why we're doing it and how it can help them improve both their own writing and the writing of

---

I do not know whether or not I will ever find a solution to all of the problems I face in the classroom, but I know I will continue to look for new ways to deal with them. I believe an important part of experiencing the writing project has been discovering that I am not alone in this frustration and that there are people who are struggling with issues similar to my own. I enjoy the stimulus provided by the writing projects and only wish this could remain a continual force throughout my teaching career. Knowing that there are no longer any writing project workshops left for me to attend leaves me feeling a bit abandoned and bereft.

—Eileen

others. The idea of talking to the students about why we're doing something is one I picked up from my experience with Dave. I could always justify peer response to colleagues or administrators, but I had never thought about justifying it to my students until one of my talks with Dave. As I recall, I was bemoaning the fact that the students' responses to one another's writing were shallow and not at all helpful. Dave asked me what exactly I was looking for, and so I told him. His response was something on the order of: "Why not tell the students what you've just told me?" I did just that before subsequent peer responding sessions, and it has helped a great deal. Many students remain shallow in their responses, but we keep working on it and steady improvement is showing. We also use peer response on a schoolwide basis in our Sustained Silent Reading and Writing (SSRW) program. Another of my tasks in the junior high is to administer SSRW. I have introduced peer response to the junior high staff as a way for them to ease the burden of reading the papers generated in their daily SSRW groups. Not only have my own classes benefited from my involvement with Dave Wilson's research, but the entire student body and school staff has also reaped the benefits whether they realize it or not.

Yet another change in my methods since that fateful semester is the increase in the number of pieces of student writing that I publish in one form or another. My classes now put together a writing booklet each semester in which every student has a piece of his or her writing published for parents, teachers, and other students to read. We have also been sending many more pieces to various magazines for consideration. While our success in being published has not been overwhelming, the fact that so many students are willing to make the attempt and to risk rejection is encouraging to me. It's a sign that the students are becoming more and more comfortable with themselves as writers. I am also attempting to select and post more writing on the bulletin boards in my room. Finding the time to type, copy, and post writing on a daily basis is difficult at best, but the addition of a computer, monitor, and printer for the exclusive use of the language arts classes this fall has been a great help.

I mentioned earlier an experiment I tried during one of Dave's visits to my class, that of reading aloud to the students. That experiment has blossomed into a regular part of my language arts curriculum. I now read short stories to my classes frequently, and I also read one longer work at some time during the school year. Oral readings are always followed by a brief journal writing time and then either small group or large group discussions about the story. This activity has begun to encourage students to read aloud to the class occasionally, usually something they themselves have written. One

The time since Dave's visits has been marked by continued change. Some of that change has been in me personally, some in the school environment and certainly in the students themselves.

Sometimes I wonder how much my changing affects my teaching and therefore my students. I rarely write in a journal; one notebook has lasted the past two years! I used to write alongside my students during writing days in class, but it became easier to increasingly give up the writing to get other things done: responding to papers, editing papers, preparation, etc. I began to feel less caught up, and the needs of church, family, and home have certainly become priorities in my life. I wanted to give more time to the Lord, to my husband, to parents struggling with illness. I grew weary of being a teacher because I couldn't get it all together or keep it all together from 8 a.m. to 4 p.m. Teaching language arts was a full-time and full-time overtime job for me. I continued to use the writing project philosophy with my writing classes, but the deeply felt connection was fading. My response to writing was strong at year's or semester's start, but it gradually dwindled to minimal positive and specific remarks. I grew tired of giving so much and struggled to keep up. Yet, if it wasn't worth doing well, it wasn't worth doing. I didn't want my students to suffer because of my lack of enthusiasm, but I was losing my desire, my joy for teaching; and a few students who were also close friends could sense this change in me.

The school environment also continued to change: more negativism crept in; turnover in administration and lack of genuine interest in the writing process or implementing writing project principles into all areas of the curriculum discouraged me. I began to feel a lack of solid focus or direction in where we as a district were headed.

I definitely experienced changes in students. Certainly I continued to enjoy success and discovery with many motivated writers, but I also began to experience more "surface" writers, those who wanted the credit, the points, the passing grade, but who did not intend to fully explore the possibilities of expressive writing. This created conflict, two opposing sides, the motivated writer-responder versus the unmotivated writer-responder. The motivated were frustrated and felt cheated. The unmotivated resented encouragement to dig deeper into their writing and responding. Discussions of writing became less focused, in-class conferencing dwindled, attempts to publish writing decreased.

I question my responsibility for the changes and assume that my fading connection with the writing and the students through my journaling impaired my ability to focus and to motivate. Perhaps fewer classes, fewer students, fewer extra-curricular duties, less busyness would have kept me at it, but I made the decision that I needed to be less busy, needed to get my priorities straight and therefore resigned my teaching position.

—Robin

of my goals is to help my students become better listeners as well as better writers. While Dave was visiting me, I also did some experimentation with having my students share, a sort of junior high version of show-and-tell, and I am continuing to develop that concept. My goal for sharing time is to have students share their own writing. Realization of that goal seems far in the future at this point, but I'm willing to wait for everything to finally fall into place. Both these ideas, that of teachers reading aloud to their students and that of sharing time, have been incorporated into SSRW as well as into my own language arts classes.

Have these changes in my style worked? Am I a better teacher now than I was before the writing project and Dave Wilson entered my life? Are my students writing better and learning more about their language? I am convinced that the answer to all these questions is a resounding *Yes!* Much of that answer is based on personal feelings and personal observations of the progress I feel my students make under the new me. I have also read in more than a few student journals comments showing that students are beginning to feel better about themselves and to have more confidence in themselves and in their writing. And believe it or not, my students make fewer and fewer grammatical, usage, and spelling mistakes as the year goes on.

One example of how students feel about my present teaching practices can be shown in the following anecdote. I recently had a particularly difficult class made up primarily of boys who disliked school with a passion and who were as rude, obnoxious, and disrespectful as I could imagine. Finally the day came when I could stand no more. For that one class, I put the desks in my room back into rows instead of my normal semi-circular arrangement, and I handed out the English textbooks that had been gathering dust on my shelves. For about a month, that class did language drills. They wrote out dozens of sentences, took tests and quizzes, and generally "learned" English the way I had taught it early in my English-teaching career. (Thank goodness Dave didn't have to witness that!) And that class, without exception, hated it. Upon concluding the unit I had selected for this class, I told them that we would go back to what everyone else in the ninth grade was doing if they thought

I know that the highlights, the mountaintops of my twelve years as a teacher have been the "connections" and the friendships I have made through writing and responding to writing. Jim Davis, Cleo Martin and the Iowa Writing Project opened that door for me. We don't write or learn about writing exclusively in an English class. I'm thankful that I've discovered that writing is a part of my life.

—Robin

they could handle it. They jumped at the opportunity, and after that whenever anyone began to get out of line, I would hear someone say, "Come on, guys, shape up or we'll have to go back to the book again." That class was manageable for the rest of the year.

But perhaps the best witness to the way students feel about my present teaching practices are the notes I received from ninth graders on the last day of school in June. My students said things like: "Thanks for all the time you spend with people and reading their writings, especially encouraging people to be open in their writing and not to be ashamed of what they write," and "Thanks for all the writing tips and the help in French. My writing matured a lot this year. Thanks!" and "I really enjoyed your classes. This was the first time I enjoyed English, because we didn't have to work out of a book. I liked the comments you put on my 'novel.' Some gave me ideas, while others inspired me to write instead of quitting. Thanks for everything you taught me!"

And my thanks to Dave Wilson and his research project. I continue to see him sitting in my classroom every period of every day. I continue to justify to him, in my mind, the things I do in that classroom. My practices have changed immensely in the past few years, and they continue to change, to approach more and more the beliefs I first expounded on that questionnaire so long ago. And best of all, my students are becoming better writers and learning to use their language better and better all the time. My days of apologizing are over.

Chapter Eight

Reflections

Almost three months after completing my final visits to the class-rooms of Robin, Wilma, Eileen, and Hal, I presented my initial results at a Conference on College Composition and Communication. I was apprehensive; it was my first solo presentation at a national conference. Wendy Bishop was on the panel with me; I remember pleasantly being surprised at the parallels between her own study of change with college writing teachers (1988) and my work, and the delightful conversation we had in the room when all others had left. But I remember more painfully the responses to my paper from two of the audience members. They insisted that I was teacher bashing.

I was horrified. It was not then nor is it now my intention to denigrate these teachers. I continue to feel humbled by the hospital-ity with which they greeted me in their homes and classrooms. The time I spent with them was enjoyable and educative; it brought me to care about and respect them. I do believe that it is important to celebrate their successes and the successes of the writing project. As a project graduate, a project instructor, and a friend, I take pride and satisfaction in these successes.

I also, however, feel a kind of responsibility that arises from my role as a project instructor, a responsibility to look more closely at teachers and our post-project lives. In reading these teachers' ques-tionnaire responses, listening to them in interviews, and observing them in their classrooms, I came to believe that the points of disso-nance, the problem areas, were as instructive—if not more instructive—than the points of consonance, the areas of success. It is at these points of dissonance that we can see most clearly the mismatches that may exist between the meaning systems of those who conduct the writing projects and those who participate in them.

Janet Emig (1983) reminds us that it is "magical thinking" to expect that students will learn directly what we teach them. The same is no doubt true of teachers who become students in a writing project or any other staff development or post-graduate program. Teachers are complex human beings, not passive receptors of knowledge. We filter experiences, like the writing project, through complicated meaning systems or personal constructs based on elements like prior experience, individual identity, and perceived social context. Our development and change, then, is messy and idiosyncratic; it reflects a mix of affect and cognition.

Robert Parker (1988) drew on the work of George Kelly (1955, 1963) and C. T. Patrick Diamond (1982a, 1982b, 1982c, 1983, 1985) to characterize personal theories and their role in change:

> ... private, personal theories ... both control and liberate the teachers who hold them. ... [A] person's constructs "channelize" her choices, decisions, and actions within particular areas of experience. These constructs form sets of pathways along which the person takes action and interprets events. A person's networks of personal constructs, which can be construed as her personal theory, controls her thought and actions. And, to the extent that a person's constructs are unarticulated and unexamined, or are impermeable, that person is locked into particular ways of acting and interpreting the world. On the other hand, if a person's constructs are permeable, and, if they are articulated and examined, that person may undertake a liberating reconstruction of her perspective. (Diamond 1988, 24–25)

Any change that comes about as a result of participation in a writing project comes about because a given teacher's constructs are permeable or because there's a fit between the meaning system promoted by the project and that held and acted on by the teacher.

Change

Results from the questionnaires indicate that these writing project graduates believe that their teaching was greatly changed by their participation in the project. Over two-thirds of them believe that such changes occurred at a degree of 75 percent or more. These teachers also valued these changes highly; almost two-thirds of them found them to be "very valuable." The twenty teachers interviewed indicated that they often perceived this change process as dramatic, and even traumatic, and that it often began during the institute, involving steps such as resistance, conversion, and continued uncertainty.

When these teachers spoke of the writing project as a facilitator of their change, they mentioned the friendship and closeness that had developed rather than the research they had read. Bonnie Sunstein (1991), in her rich study of teachers during a writing project, borrows from anthropologist Victor Turner (1982) to understand the peculiar temporary culture and fellowship of a summer writing project. Turner calls this fellowship "communitas"; it arises in part from the suspended nature of a "liminal" event "when the past is momentarily negated, suspended, or abrogated, and the future has not yet begun." All things seem possible in this time; it is "an instant of pure potentiality."

For three weeks in the summer many of the responsibilities of these teachers' lives are suspended; they live in a temporary literate community where relationships feel tight and deep and dreaming is both possible and encouraged. Freed temporarily of the realities of their lives in schools, teachers are able to imagine and hope for other possibilities. Such hope and imagination may be essential contributing elements of their perceived change.

When the teachers from this study spoke of change, they also spoke of religious conversion. This metaphor is not surprising; these teachers perceived this change as a surrendering of an old life, a shaking loose from the past, and an acquisition of "a new vision" and a new "community." Other researchers, most notably Wendy Bishop (1990) and Kathy Boardman (1992), have found English-trained teacher/students using similar conversion metaphors. Innovations are acts of faith; perhaps, then, because these teachers came to the writing project of their own will and with a felt need, and because of the community, catharsis, and success they felt as participants in the project, particularly in the afternoon workshops, they could more easily hold such faith. While these teachers' "sense of euphoria" and "new birth" may make outsiders—and some insiders—skeptical, just as they did me when I first met project graduates like Jerie, Lin, Tom, and Sandra, these feelings are genuine and may play an essential role in helping launch the teachers back into their own classrooms and contexts with the strength, energy, and conviction necessary for change making.

This metaphor of religious conversion, though, is problematic. It suggests sin and error, perceptions Robin claimed in Chapter Three in her talk of "being sinful" in her post-project use of a traditional grammar textbook. Such talk posits teaching practices as either sinful or virtuous and the writing project as a kind of external moral authority and redeemer. Conversion implies a sudden change, an emptying of the self, rather than a kind of stuttering, subjective process of negotiation over time, which seems closer to the experience of these writing project graduates.

Their talk about their beliefs and practices; my observations in the classrooms of Robin, Wilma, Eileen, and Hal; and my own experience as a project graduate suggest that teacher constructs may often be more prone to change—more permeable—in areas like topic choice, journal use, positive teacher response, and peer response.

As I indicated in Chapter Three, these project graduates seemed especially eager to surrender control and allow for more student choice in the area of writing topics. Most of these teachers never enjoyed feeling responsible for finding topics for their students, especially since their students often seemed disappointed in these teacher-assigned topics. "Why let that be in my lap?" Louise exclaimed.

Their use of journals and their positive response to student writing seemed to be consonant with the teachers' beliefs and with the seven writing project principles. The journals provided an opportunity for frequent student and teacher writing, free of teacher control and the constraints of language conventions. Sometimes, as with the conferences, journals became a place for students to reflect on their writing and writing processes. The journals also allowed for a ritualistic way of begining class—of getting the students settled and centered after their commute from lunch, study hall, or various classes. They provided the teachers with some quiet time to take attendance and then do a bit of their own writing; they provided a kind of sanctuary in teachers' busy days.

Robin, Wilma, Eileen, and Hal became readers for their students, responding positively and specifically to their writing, creating environments that encouraged and affirmed those efforts. All used green ink and wrote marginal and end note comments on their students' papers, practices they borrowed from their writing project instructors.

Peer response, although frequently used, was more troublesome. The teachers' intentions here were to provide their writers with more readers who could help them build on their strengths. Ideally, peer response also liberates the teacher from being the sole reader of all student work. But the results were mixed. Initial teacher response and the display of student writing seemed to work well. Later, however, the teachers and students sometimes had to cope with negative, shallow, and flippant responses that may have been a consequence of the students' attitudes, ages, and uncertainty about their role as responders and the swiftness with which the teachers introduced peer response. The problems with peer response may also have arisen, in part, from students' realization of the real economy of their classrooms; the teacher's assessment of student work was more highly valued given his or her institutional role as grader.

And grading is one area in which the study suggests these teachers' constructs were less permeable. Other areas include "correctness," form, and the importance of quietness in a classroom. Here a kind of general instructional disharmony resulted from the teachers being haunted by opposing beliefs and notions of accountability and responsibility. They wanted their students to control their own writing. They believed that writing is valuable and that attention to meaning rather than to standard conventions of language is more important. At the same time, they also believed that they had to assign and justify a grade for writing; they felt responsible for teaching literature "and other stuff"; and they felt "accountable for the correctness" of their students' writing.

In Chapter Four I cited Richard Young's (1978, 31) description of the traditional paradigm of writing and writing instruction:

> The overt features . . . are obvious enough: the emphasis on the composed product rather than the composing process; the analysis of discourse into words, sentences, and paragraphs; the classification of discourse into description, narration, exposition, and argument; the strong concern with usage (syntax, spelling, punctuation) and with style (economy, clarity, emphasis); the preoccupation with the informal essay and the research paper; and so on.

Maxine Hairston (1982, 78) has more to say about this traditional paradigm:

> First, its adherents believe that competent writers know what they are going to say before they begin to write; thus their most important task when they are preparing to write is finding a form into which to organize their content. They also believe . . . that teaching editing is teaching writing.

Form and correctness are central elements of this traditional paradigm. Given that and these teachers' years of experience in that paradigm—both as students and as teachers—and the pervasive presence of that paradigm in our culture, it is not surprising that form and correctness should appear as two areas of dissent or dissonance. There is much in these teachers' pasts, in their institutions, and in our culture to suggest that form and correctness are central to good writing instruction and thus to make these constructs less permeable, less prone to change.

Any change that came about did so because the teachers' constructs changed. The liminal nature of the writing project and the flash of "communitas" that developed there may be essential contributing elements to their change in beliefs and practice. Many of these teachers attempted to reexperience that powerful but temporary culture and community by returning to other levels of the writing project.

For Robin, Wilma, Eileen, and Hal, I was a kind of embodiment of that culture and community come to visit them in their own classrooms; as Hal said, I "was the Iowa Writing Project come to life." My research project and I seemed to provoke further change.

In part this seems to have happened because they hoped to "teach up to" the writing project. My presence, they claimed, validated their efforts, reinforced their credibility, and gave them further incentive to bring belief and practice closer together. Hal's "experiment" with his second-period class—an attempt at not "being discovered for the fraud" he felt he was—ended up persuading him that he could put more of his beliefs into practice.

And in part, this seems to have happened because my presence and my questions provoked these teachers to articulate and examine some of their personal constructs, allowing them to do as Parker (1988) suggests and "undertake a liberating reconstruction" of their perspectives.

Implications

As Rob said, "When you go through the project you get this sense of community and you see this growth in your peers and it's not hard to imagine what the growth would be like in kids. And that's going to help you go back to the classroom more confidently and interject some of those same approaches." The workshops gave the teachers a new approach and direct experience that such an approach could work. This facilitated surface change—change at Fullan's (1982) "materials" and "approaches" levels. New "rituals" developed—green ink, journals, writing folders, conferences, responsive marginal and end comments—along with a new vocabulary—"process," "polish," "ownership," "draft"—all of which identified one as a member of a new community, an Iowa Writing Project process community. Teachers are often tired, busy, and lonely people; we hunger for such membership.

At the same time, those aspects of teachers' contexts that contributed to their fatigue and isolation may also guarantee that any change remains at this surface level. Old assumptions may simply be replaced or joined by new and perhaps contradictory ones; a lack of time for reflection and a separation from the new community keep these assumptions buried and unexamined. Ultimately this can be crippling.

Clearly their participation in the writing project has had a strong continuing influence on these teachers. Their new belief systems about writing and the teaching of writing, their successes in enacting most parts of those belief systems, and the degree to which those beliefs—held and enacted—are consonant with the seven writing project principles serve as evidence of that influence. Such an influence, however, has not yet enabled these teachers to exorcise old conceptions. As successful as they are, they are still haunted by contradictory beliefs about writing, teaching, and the teaching of writing, and thus they live with dissonance.

To describe these points of apparent dissonance is not to blame teachers for any "failures." Teachers teach as we do because we hold certain beliefs and assumptions about our roles and responsibilities. These beliefs and assumptions are not always made explicit; they come not just from our work in education courses or staff development workshops, but also from our years of experience as students in elementary, secondary, and college classrooms, and from our memberships in a culture that values objectivity, quantification, and generalization. These assumptions reside and are promoted in *Time* and *Newsweek*, in popular literature, in television sitcoms, and in depictions that have become commonplace of teachers and schools. Like other social and linguistic structures that serve to shore up the status quo, popular cultural assumptions about education function as a given, as a "natural" or inevitable state of things. They provide the very structures with which teachers conceptualize our work. In this way, these assumptions and beliefs also serve as constraints, setting the parameters for the field of beliefs and practices in which teaching and learning can be conceptualized. Their presence as a "given" in so much of our experience renders them powerful and difficult to see or subvert.

If teachers are to change and feel successful in their change, they must be given time. They must be supported in their risk taking. They must be given opportunities to reflect on and talk about their experiences and to articulate and revise their assumptions. There may be, however, a "natural" dissonance between theory and practice that assures that one of the two must change. Even given the time, support, and opportunities, it may be that teachers will have to live with such dissonance until they are able to reconceptualize their roles as teachers or their notions of what it means to teach writing as a "process." We can help them do that by provoking and supporting them to articulate and examine their personal constructs.

Teachers will interpret and act on the writing project within the constraints of those personal constructs. In order to assist teachers in their efforts at changing during and after their participation in a writing project or another staff development or post-graduate program, we need to help them make those constructs more permeable. We can do this by prompting and encouraging them to tell stories. As Joy Ritchie and I have discovered in a study of preservice teachers

(1993), ". . . telling our stories is an 'original, critical instrument' for articulating and revising all of our experience." Teachers need to be given repeated opportunities to compose, reflect on, and critique their teaching, learning, and literacy stories, which allows them to begin to see their own constructs and mobilize their experiences consciously, to integrate them into their working conceptions of writing, learning, and teaching. In doing this we assist teachers in taking greater control over their own change processes.

For Robin, Wilma, Eileen, and Hal that stuttering, subjective process of negotiation—change—continues; they are not now as I've painted them here. And I continue to learn. This past summer I worked with twenty-five teachers in the Nebraska Writing Project, listening to them compose their personal and professional life histories, marveling at the similarities and differences between the Iowa and Nebraska Projects.

I wonder what I would find if I were to follow Sarah, Rob, or Jan—one of these new Nebraska Writing Project graduates—back into their classrooms?

Appendix: Methodology

This study examined the ways in which participation in the Iowa Writing Project has had a continuing influence on those secondary English teachers who studied in the Iowa Writing Project in 1982 and 1985. Four specific questions guided the research. First, as determined from questionnaires distributed to all 1982 and 1985 IWP participants who teach secondary English, what is their assessment of the influence which participation in the IWP has had on their teaching? Second, as determined from interviews with twenty questionnaire respondents, why have these teachers responded as they have concerning the influence which the IWP has had on their teaching? Third, what evidence will the case studies (of four teachers selected from the larger sample) reveal of the continuing influence of the IWP? Finally, what relationships can be found between the four case study teachers and the larger sample regarding the influence that participation in the IWP had on their teaching?

To answer these questions, I collected data in three stages. In the first stage I distributed a questionnaire to all 1982 and 1985 IWP participants who teach secondary English. This questionnaire provided background information for the rest of the study and asked these teachers to assess the IWP's continuing influence on their teaching. In the second stage, a follow-up to the first, I interviewed twenty respondents to learn why they had assessed the IWP's continuing influence as they had, and to learn more about the contexts in which these teachers were operating. The final stage employed observational and case study techniques to describe the teaching practices of four of the interviewees.

The Design of the Study

Participants

In 1982 the Iowa Writing Project ran five Level I institutes around the state; in 1985 Level I institutes were held at eleven sites. Working with the instructors of these institutes and from the lists of participants, I identified the forty 1982 participants and the seventy-five 1985 participants who were teaching secondary English.

Table 2
Participant Profile: All Teachers

Years Experience before IWP

	mean	SD
Respondents (N = 79)	10.6	6.2
Interviewees (N = 20)	9.5	5.2
Case Studies (N = 4)	8.3	5.7

Highest Degree Attained	BA/BS (%)	MA/MS (%)	PhD (%)
Respondents (N = 79)	65.8	32.9	1.3
Interviewees (N = 20)	75	25	0
Case Studies (N = 4)	100	0	0

Teaching Assignment grades:	7–8 (%)	9–12 (%)	7–12 (%)
Respondents (N = 79)	19	62	19
Interviewees (N = 20)	15	55	30
Case Studies (N = 4)	0	50	50

Number Workshops Taken	1 (%)	2 (%)	3 (%)	4 (%)
Respondents (N = 79)	70.9	16.5	11.4	1.3
Interviewees (N = 20)	30	40	25	5
Case Studies (N = 4)	0	50	50	0

As indicated in Table 2, those IWP participants who responded (75 percent) had, on the average, over ten years (10.6) of teaching experience prior to enrolling in their first IWP summer institute. Seventy-one percent (70.9 percent) of the respondents had taken only one level of the writing project; 16.5 percent had taken two levels; 11.4 percent had studied in three levels; and one teacher (1.3 percent) reported having taken four levels: He took the first three and then recently repeated level one.

Almost two-thirds of the respondents (65.8 percent) had only bachelor's degrees and just over one-third (34.2 percent) had earned master's degrees. One teacher in this last category had earned two bachelor's degrees, a master's degree, and a doctorate. His first three degrees were in social studies but the third, a bachelor of arts in writing, was awarded just two years prior to his taking Level I of the IWP. Most of the teachers reported that their degree work was in language-related areas—English, reading, speech, communication—not surprising since all do at least part of their teaching in secondary English/language arts.

Sixty-two percent of the respondents (62.0 percent) reported that their teaching assignments fall within grades nine through twelve. Nineteen percent (19.0 percent) taught within grades seven and eight; an equal percentage (19.0 percent) had assignments that had them teaching a range of classes between grades seven and twelve.

Using the results from Stage One, I selected ten 1982 respondents who represented the range of questionnaire respondents in terms of years of teaching experience, grade levels taught, size of district, highest degree attained, site of original writing project, and number of subsequent projects taken. Ten 1985 respondents were chosen on a similar basis.

These twenty teachers had, on the average, about one year less teaching experience prior to enrolling in their first writing project institute than did the larger sample of questionnaire respondents from which they were drawn (9.5 versus 10.6 years). On the other hand, they had more experience with the Iowa Writing Project than that larger sample. Thirty percent of the interviewees had taken only one level of the writing project; 40 percent had taken only two levels; 25 percent had studied in only three levels; and, again, one teacher (5 percent), Matt, reported having taken four levels (he repeated Level I after taking the other three). Consistent with the larger sample, 75 percent of the interviewees had only bachelor's degrees, and 25 percent had earned master's degrees.

The teaching assignments of these interviewees were also reasonably consistent with those held by the questionnaire respondents. Fifteen percent of the interviewees reported that their teaching assignments fell within grades seven and eight; 55 percent fell within grades nine through twelve; 30 percent had assignments that had them teaching a range of classes between grades seven and twelve.

From the twenty interviewees of Stage Two, two 1982 and two 1985 IWP participants were selected for case studies and classroom observations. I sought teachers whose teaching contexts had changed the least since the years immediately preceeding their involvement in the project, whose schools were located within sixty miles of the University of Iowa, and who most expressed an interest in the questions raised by the study and a willingness to work with me in answering those questions. In addition, I was able to select four teachers whose teaching assignments had them working at the ninth-grade level, thus providing the study with a tighter focus. A profile of these teachers appears in Chapter Five.

To achieve an even richer picture of what happens in these four classrooms, I selected two case study students—one male and one female—for each teacher-participant. Students were chosen on the basis of their willingness to participate and their level of success in the classes observed as based on the teachers' recommendations.

To select the students, I spoke to each of the teachers' classes for about ten minutes. During the presentation I explained the study as a whole and asked for volunteers who were willing to meet for two half-hour interviews outside of class and who were willing to share their writing drafts and processes with me over the course of the semester of observation. I then passed around a sheet on which volunteers listed their names, their home phone numbers, and any times outside of class that were convenient for them to meet with me. From the lists of volunteers for each site and with the help of my teacher-participants, I made a preliminary selection of one male and one female student per site. I then contacted these students individually, confirming their willingness to participate, and received written permission for their participation from their parents/guardians.

In all cases the students chosen were cited by their teachers as being either "good" writers or "prolific" writers, and in all cases the females turned out to be more assertive and self-assured than their male counterparts.

Procedures

The questionnaire I designed sought information in four areas. Part I provided baseline information on these IWP participants: teaching assignments, consistency of teaching situations, years of experience, degrees earned, professional involvement, and continuing involvement with the IWP. Part II was drawn from a study into the "Effects on Student Writing of Teacher Training in the National Writing Project Model" (Pritchard, 1987) and focused on teacher behaviors. Respondents were asked to estimate the amount of time given to their own writing, sharing of writing, and talk about the teaching of writing. Part III included nine items that were based on implications of the seven IWP principles mentioned in Chapter One; these items asked the respondents to report the extent to which they follow these implications in the classes in which they were making the most concerted effort to teach writing. The other two items in Part III asked these teachers to assess the degree to which their participation in the IWP had changed their teaching and to assign a value to these changes. The final section of the questionnaire was comprised of four open-ended questions that invited the respondents to write briefly about their efforts at teaching writing, problems they have with implementing writing as fostered by the IWP, and their beliefs about writing and the teaching of writing.

To test my questionnaire, I sent a version to each of four secondary English teachers who participated in the Project in 1981. I asked them to complete the questionnaire, record the time it took them to do so, and to note any items that gave them troubles. All reported that it took them between fifteen and twenty minutes to answer it; none had any problems in doing so.

The questionnaires, along with cover letters and return envelopes, were mailed to the one hundred fifteen 1982 and 1985 IWP participants who had been identified as being secondary English teachers. Follow-up letters were sent to those who failed to respond within three weeks. Seventy-five percent of the questionnaires were completed and returned.

To explore the "why" behind these teachers' questionnaire responses, I interviewed each of the twenty teachers selected for stage two once. Questions were designed to draw a clearer picture of these teachers, the contexts in which they operate, their classroom practices, their beliefs about writing and the teaching of writing, and the ways in which they believe they have been influenced by their participation in the IWP. Specific questions evolved from each of the teachers' specific questionnaire responses. In addition, I asked for further elaboration whenever a teacher's interview responses indicated that such elaboration was necessary or would be helpful. These interviews were audiotaped for later analysis.

To determine what it was these teachers do in their classrooms, I observed each of the four case study teachers for several full days and then together we selected one ninth-grade class for closer study and observation. Observational and case study methodologies enable one to see the complexities of the classrooms, the interactions that take place there, the people who interact there, and the broader contexts in which the classrooms operate. My visits were scheduled in advance. Aside from the first visit when I was introduced and from the visit later when I appealed for case study students, my visits involved virtually no disruption of normal classroom operations. During each visit I sat in the back of the room, taking field notes, talking informally with students before and after class, but not participating in any classroom activities. I spent a total of seventy-two hours in these four teachers' classrooms.

My field notes attempted to record what happens in each class— what the teachers said and what they had the students do. In addition I periodically asked the teachers about their intentions for a specific class before it met or to give me a retrospective examination of a class after the students had left. Immediately after each day of observation I annotated and clarified my field notes for the general patterns that seemed to be emerging.

The eight case study students were special focuses of my attention in my classroom observations. In addition, I interviewed each student twice and collected copies of all of the class writing done by each student. The first interview drew from Part III of the questionnaire from Stage One and asked the students to report what it was they believed was happening in the classes observed and what it was they believed their teacher-participants believed about writing and the teaching of writing. The second interview revolved around a piece of writing done for class and asked the students to talk about the processes and drafts that led up to the final product. Specific questions evolved from each of the students' specific responses. In addition, I asked for further elaboration whenever a student's interview responses indicated that such elaboration was necessary or would be helpful. These interviews were audiotaped for later analysis.

Analysis

The results from Parts II and III of the questionnaire were quantified to create a statistical picture of the respondents' classroom practices. To the extent that it was possible, the results from Part I were also quantified; this in order to paint a preliminary portrait of the study participants. I analyzed the content of the teachers' responses to the four items in Part IV.

Tapes of the twenty interviews were transcribed and examined, particularly in terms of their relationships with the questionnaire responses and the seven IWP principles. The results were used to paint greater detail into the portraits that emerged from Stage One of this study.

Data from the observational stage of the study was synthesized in a number of ways. I examined transcriptions of all interviews with the teachers for evidence of their belief systems about writing and the teaching of writing. I then used my field notes to identify the kinds of writing activities sponsored by each of the teachers. Transcriptions of the interviews with the students provided me with their impressions of the writing activities in which they were engaged and of the processes that preceded their written products. Portraits of each of the four teachers and their classrooms emerged. All of this, then, was set up against the seven IWP foundational statements. Relationships between these teachers' practices and beliefs and those ideas fostered by the IWP were noted. I also attempted to identify the relationships that could be found between the four case study teachers and the larger pools from which they were drawn regarding the continuing influence of participation in the IWP.

References

Bishop, Wendy. 1988. "Training Teachers of Writing: Making the Familiar Strange." Paper presented at the annual meeting of the Conference on College Composition and Communication, St. Louis, MO, 19 March.

————. 1990. *Something Old, Something New: College Writing Teachers and Classroom Change*. Carbondale, IL: Southern Illinois University Press.

Boardman, Kathy. 1992. "Teaching Experience: New Writing Instructors in a College Program." Ph.D. diss., University of Nebraska–Lincoln.

Britton, James. 1970. *Language and Learning*. Coral Gables, FL: University of Miami Press.

Britton, James, Tony Burgess, Nancy Martin, Alex McLeod, and Harold Rosen. 1975. *The Development of Writing Abilities* (11-18). London: McMillan Education Limited.

Bunch, Deborah. 1980a. "A Case Study: Sandra Bolton." Unpublished manuscript.

————. 1980b. "A Case Study: Kay Van Mantgen." Unpublished manuscript.

Daniels, Harvey, and Steven Zemelman. 1985. *A Writing Project: Training Teachers of Composition from Kindergarten to College*. Portsmouth, NH: Heinemann.

Davis, James S. 1987. Conversation with author, 17 February.

————. 1990. Conversation with author, 13 December.

Diamond, C.T. Patrick. 1982a. "Teachers Can Change: A Kellyan Interpretation." *Journal of Education for Teaching*, 8: 163–173.

————. 1982b. "Understanding Others." *International Journal of Intercultural Relations*, 6: 395–420.

————. 1982c. "'You Always End Up with Conflict': An Account of Constraints in Teaching Written Composition." In *English for the Eighties*, edited by Robert D. Eagleson. Sydney: Australian Association for the Teaching of English.

————. 1983. "Teacher Perspectives on the Teaching of Writing." *The Alberta Journal of Educational Research*, 29: 25–30.

————. 1985. "Becoming a Teacher: An Altering Eye." In *Issues and Approaches in Personal Construct Theory III*, edited by Donald Bannister. London: Academic Press.

Elbow, Peter. 1973. *Writing Without Teachers*. New York: Oxford University Press.

Emig, Janet. 1971. *The Composing Processes of Twelfth Graders.* Urbana, IL: National Council of Teachers of English.

———. 1983. "Non-Magical Thinking: Presenting Writing Developmentally in School." In *The Web of Meaning: Essays on Writing, Teaching, Learning, and Thinking.* Portsmouth, NH: Boynton/Cook.

Fullan, Michael. 1982. *The Meaning of Educational Change.* New York: Teachers College Press.

Graves, Donald. 1983. *Writing: Teachers and Children at Work.* Portsmouth, NH: Heinemann.

Hairston, Maxine. 1982. "The Winds of Change: Thomas Kuhn and the Revolution in the Teaching of Writing." *College Composition and Communication,* 33 (1): 76–88.

Kelly, George. 1955. *The Psychology of Personal Constructs.* New York: Norton.

———. 1963. *A Theory of Personality.* New York: Norton.

Macrorie, Ken. 1970. *Uptaught.* Rochelle Park, NJ: Hayden.

———. 1980. *Searching Writing.* Rochelle Park, NJ: Hayden.

Martin, Cleo. 1985. "Observations about the Teaching of Writing." Paper presented to the Iowa Association of School Boards, Des Moines, IA.

Moffett, James. 1968. *Teaching the Universe of Discourse.* Boston, MA: Houghton Mifflin Company.

———. 1981. *Coming on Center: English Education in Evolution.* Portsmouth, NH: Boynton/Cook.

Parker, Robert. 1988. "Theories of Writing Instruction: Having Them, Using Them, Changing Them." *English Education,* 20: 18–40.

Pritchard, Ruie Jane. 1987. "Effects on Student Writing of Teacher Training in the National Writing Project Model." *Written Communication* 4(1): 51–67.

Sunstein, Bonnie. 1991. "Summer Revisions: An Ethnographic Study of High School Teachers in the Culture of a Summer Writing Program." Ph.D. diss., University of New Hampshire.

Turner, Victor. 1982. *From Ritual to Theater: The Human Seriousness of Play.* New York: Performing Arts Journal Publications.

Vygotsky, Lev. 1962. *Thought and Language.* Cambridge, MA: Massachusetts Institute of Technology Press.

Wilson, David E., and Joy S. Ritchie. 1993. "Resistance and Revision: Using Narrative for Teacher Re-Education." Paper presented at the annual winter meeting of the National Council of Teachers of English Research Assembly, Chicago, 13 February.

Young, Richard. 1978. "Paradigms and Problems: Needed Research in Rhetorical Invention." In *Research on Composing,* edited by Charles R. Cooper and Lee Odell. Urbana, IL: National Council of Teachers of English.

Also available from Heinemann-Boynton/Cook . . .

Composing a Culture
Inside a Summer Writing Program with High School Teachers
Bonnie Sunstein, University of Iowa
Foreword by **Maxine Greene**

What actually happens to a teacher during a summer writing program? Why do high school teachers seem to need the support of a summer program in order to teach writing with confidence, and often against a prescribed curriculum? Why don't other kinds of inservice models affect people as much as summer programs? What is the nature of this encounter, and why see it as a temporary culture? How does a summer program affect a teacher during the summer, and then what does she bring back to school in the fall?

In *Composing a Culture*, Bonnie Sunstein attempts to answer these questions and more. Drawing on composition and feminist theory, socio-linguistics, educational philosophy and psychology, anthropology and folklore studies, she examines three combined New Hampshire writing programs which occurred during the summer of 1990.

Although this summer writing program lasts for only three weeks, it is an important event, sometimes a turning point in a teacher's career. The author documents three high school teachers' experience during the summer, listening to their stories, observing them as they worked, watching as they read and wrote and responded, listening to their complaints and triumphs as they re-thought their own literacies in the company of other teachers and writers, all teaching and writing. Each teacher needs to "read" two cultures as she understands and participates in them — that of her summer, and that of her school. Each teacher shuttles, too, between her personal agenda and the program's agenda for her. Through each teacher's tensions, actions, conversations with others, formal and informal writing, responses to reading, and the author's own observations and conversations with them, Bonnie Sunstein captures the ways each teacher interprets the summer's academic and social system.

Interspersed throughout *Composing a Culture* are five short "intertexts," meant as verbal snapshots, "landscapes of the culture itself." In each intertext the author freezes a moment just long enough to examine some of the thinking, pieces of texts, scholarship, and experience that contribute to that moment, adding flesh and color to the book.

From lectures by writers and poets to classes, peer conferences, cookouts and lobster dinners, what emerges in *Composing a Culture* is a detailed portrait of teachers coming to knowledge together in an intense three week community; a collaboration between themselves and those in their temporary world, crafted through relationships and conversations.

Boynton/Cook / 0-86709-342-0 / 1994

Also available from Heinemann-Boynton/Cook . . .

Learning Change
One School District Meets Language Across the Curriculum
Nancy B. Lester, The Write Company, and **Cynthia S. Onore**, City College, CUNY

"I recommend this thoughtful book to readers already undergoing the transition to a whole language curriculum. Their background experiences will help them to identify with the situations encountered by the Claremont School District and to appreciate the growing pains and struggles of these teachers as they changed from learners to leaders."
    —Language Arts

Learning Change grew out of the observations, reflections, and questions the authors formulated in over a decade of teaching and learning with classroom teachers through professional development programs. Specifically, it details the four year inservice program organized and directed by the authors in a school district north of New York City.

In their words, the book "examines how teachers and schools might transform themselves, why change is possible when it is, and what constraints operate in thwarting it. Our goal is to paint a picture which reflects all of the issues — personal, social, cultural, and institutional — that make up the process of change, which is more difficult, more complex, and more idiosyncratic than we ever realized. We want to show that it is, nonetheless, possible. Both teachers and institutions have the energy, resources, and flexibility to bring it about.

"We have come to believe that schools can (must) change from the bottom up — from changes in the ways individual teachers teach and learn with their students to changes in the voices and authority teachers assert in school decision-making to changes in school governance and relationships among educators at all levels in the school setting. In the end, *Learning Change* is our call for a more genuine democratic education in American schools."

Boynton/Cook / 0-86709-254-8 / 1990

Contact your local supplier, favorite bookstore, or call us direct.

Heinemann-Boynton/Cook
361 Hanover Street
Portsmouth, NH 03801-3912
(800) 541-2086

8107